TRAVELLING FOR PLEASURE

Tony Newberry.

TRAVELLING
FOR PLEASURE

Tony Newbery

GOMER

First Impression—June 1994
Second Impression—May 1995

ISBN 1 85902 111 5

Printed in Wales by
J. D. Lewis and Sons Ltd., Gomer Press, Llandysul

To Judy with love and thanks
for being so patient.

ACKNOWLEDGMENTS

Special thanks are due to Martin Eckley, without whose help this book could never have been started, and to William Condry without whose encouragement it might never have been finished.

The appendix on archaeology relies heavily on Katherine Watson's volume dealing with North Wales in the Heinemann Regional Archaeology series, and I am also indebted to Alun R. Jones and William Tydeman whose edition of Joseph Hucks's *Pedestrian Tour Through North Wales* contains new information about the author's life.

Mairwen Prys Jones of Gomer Press has made working with an editor a pleasure and her gentle goading has saved me from many errors. Those which remain are my own.

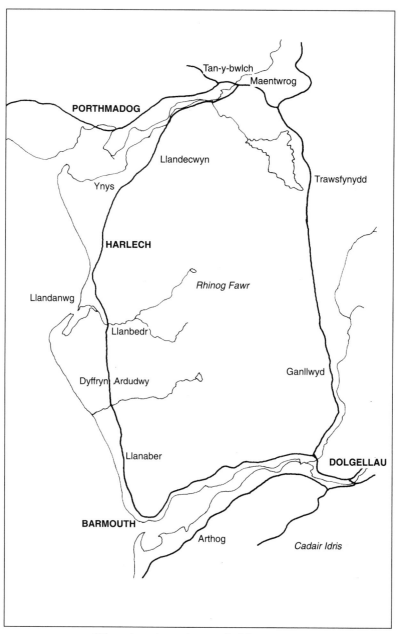

Where the early tourists travelled for pleasure.

CONTENTS

THE

CAMBRIAN
TRAVELLER'S GUIDE,

IN EVERY DIRECTION;

containing

REMARKS MADE DURING MANY EXCURSIONS,

IN

THE PRINCIPALITY OF WALES,

AND

BORDERING DISTRICTS,

augmented by

EXTRACTS FROM THE BEST WRITERS.

SECOND EDITION,

CORRECTED AND CONSIDERABLY ENLARGED

STOURPORT:
PRINTED BY THE EDITOR, AND PUBLISHED
for him by
LONGMAN, HURST, REES, ORME & BROWN;
SHERWOOD, NEELY, & JONES; AND BALDWIN, CRADOCK & JOY,
LONDON.
1813.

[Entered at Stationers' Hall.]

George Nicholson's pioneering guide-book.

PREFACE

*'The characters of nature are legible; but it is difficult
for those who run, to read them'.*
Edmund Burke 1729-97

There can be few visitors to North Wales who do not at some time wonder, as they travel through our still beautiful countryside, how it looked in the past. This book, based on the writings of tourists who visited Ardudwy during the late eighteenth and early nineteenth centuries, should help to satisfy this curiosity.

We are fortunate that two hundred years ago it was fashionable for tourists to keep a journal, and if possible to have it published. As a result a large body of writing exists which provides us with a detailed record of what this part of North Wales looked like between 1790 and 1850. For those who would like to follow in the footsteps of these early tourists, this material provides an opportunity to see the area through their eyes. The reader can share the delights of those arduous journeys without having to endure all the hardships.

This is not an attempt at a nostalgic re-creation of a lost age of pastoral bliss; but it does offer both the modern visitor and inhabitants of the area some new perspectives, and an opportunity to see Ardudwy in the context of the changes which have taken place during the last two centuries. Though much has changed, much also remains the same, and by being selective in one's travels it is still possible to experience an older Wales without stirring very far from the comforts which later developments have provided. Our predecessors were much concerned with what they called 'quietude', meaning rest, calm and tranquillity. This quality is still available in abundance in Ardudwy for those who know where, and how, to find it.

The area we are dealing with extends from the Vale of Ffestiniog in the north to Cadair Idris in the south, and as far inland as a line drawn roughly from Dolgellau through Trawsfynydd. Cardigan Bay forms a natural western boundary, and it is the contrast which exists between the vast seascapes of the coastline and the wall of mountains which extends almost to the shore, which makes this relatively small area one of the most visually exciting in Britain. Within it lie three distinct areas corresponding to the three levels of influence which man has exerted on the landscape. The coastal fringe has been developed over the last two hundred years to provide all the facilities necessary for a viable rural economy. Slightly further inland, on the lower slopes of the mountains and in the beds of the valleys, we see an

agricultural landscape which has changed little since the end of the eighteenth century. This is a world of small fields enclosed by stone walls, and of native oak woods; a landscape of great beauty which is essentially man made. The open moorlands and rocky precipices which form a stark background to these mellow foothills have changed little since Giraldus Cambrensis, author of Archbishop Baldwin's *Itinerary through Wales,* recorded his impressions when he passed this way in 1188. Although we tend to see these mountain areas as wilderness, the influence of man has been exerted here at least since the dawn of recorded history, but in a form so benign as to be unobtrusive.

The Hundred of Ardudwy does not extend south of the Mawddach estuary, and strictly speaking Dolgellau and Cadair Idris lie outside its geographical boundary; however they are so important to the area that I have included them. It would be virtually impossible to consider the Mawddach Estuary without mentioning Cadair Idris, the northern precipices of which form a natural boundary. It was the chance of seeing this mountain, and climbing to its summit, which brought many of the early tourists to the area. Dolgellau was the main centre for their activities.

The book is divided into three sections. The first chapter provides a background to the writings of the early tourists and also some other travellers who preceded them, but who were not visiting Wales strictly for pleasure. It considers their reasons for coming here and their attitudes to the landscape and to the Welsh people, their culture and their way of life. In the following five chapters we move northwards through Ardudwy using extracts from their journals, and from some early guidebooks, to describe the area in a way that makes it easy to find the places which the authors are writing about, and also providing more specific information for the modern tourist. This includes descriptions of some not too arduous walks. An appendix at the back of the book suggests longer and more demanding excursions which can only be made on foot, and which offer the opportunity to see Ardudwy in the same way as the early tourists; travelling slowly, through wild and often remote country. Another appendix provides brief biographical notes on some of the authors whose work has been quoted.

The pronunciation of Welsh place names (Appendix III) can cause some problems for visitors, but this is not nearly as difficult as it may seem when you are first confronted with a seemingly endless succession of consonants. For those who are not familiar with Wales, the few minutes it will take to read this before starting on the rest of the book will be amply repaid. It is easier to remember names once you have learned to pronounce them, and you will save yourself, and the local people you will meet, much frustration. In the days before road signs and reliable maps, the spelling of Welsh place names presented great problems to the early tourists. Their brave attempts are often so distorted as to cause confusion, so where necessary I have inserted a 'translation' in brackets. The spellings used in the rest of the text are accepted modern forms which will be easily recognisable to those who do not speak the Welsh Language. Therefore Barmouth is used rather than the Welsh name Abermaw (or Bermo) but Dolgellau is preferred to the anglicised Dolgelley.

Tourists' impressions of the country through which they travel are often superficial, though this limitation is usually mitigated by the objectivity and enthusiasm which a fresh eye brings to their descriptions. Unfortunately the very unfamiliarity which makes this possible can lead to inaccuracies which are all too obvious to locals; those who know Ardudwy well may notice some in the extracts which are quoted. Corrections to the most flagrant of these are provided in the adjoining text.

Finally, a short note about the word 'tourist'. According to the Oxford English Dictionary this term first became current in 1780, when it was used in the advertisement for a book about the Lake District: 'He throws the piece only into the way of the actual tourist.' The definition is given as; 'one who travels for pleasure or culture, visiting a number of places for their objects of interest, scenery, culture or the like.' In our own time the term seems to have taken on an almost derogatory tone. Throughout this book it is used in the strict sense of the definition, which should offend no-one.

CHAPTER 1

THE EARLY TOURISTS

John Torbuck was not a tourist, nor does his book *A Collection of Welsh Travels and Memories of Wales*, published in 1738, give any hint that he derived much pleasure from his visit to this beautiful country. A London lawyer with a sarcastic wit, he presents a picture of the Principality which, though it might cause indignation today, would have seemed quite appropriate at the time.

> Having had the Honour to be employed in a Negotiation between an English Gentleman and the Ancient Britons, I was not only upon the Borders, and (as it were) the Limbs of Wales, but have travelled through the very Bowels of the Country . . .
>
> The Country looks like the fag End of the Creation; the very Rubbish of Noah's Flood; and will (if anything) serve to confirm an Epicurean in his Creed, That the world was made by Chance.

This extract from his often very amusing memoir provides a good example of the feelings inspired in travellers, before the industrial revolution, when they were confronted with what we would now describe as wild and beautiful scenery. At that time there were many who still believed that mountainous areas were the result of the original smooth surface of the earth being deformed by the upwelling of waters during Noah's Flood. Even in the nineteenth century similar, if less intemperate views, were still being expressed by visitors who were confronted by such landscapes. Yet, less than half a century after Torbuck's outburst, Thomas Pennant, a Welshman who had travelled extensively on the continent, had little difficulty in recognising the charms of this part of Wales.

By the end of the eighteenth century a spate of travel books extolling the beauties of Wales were persuading ever growing numbers of people to visit the very places which had so repelled Torbuck. By the end of the nineteenth century, upland areas which remained relatively unpopulated, were a magnet for mountaineers and hill-walkers as well as for less energetic tourists who would drive into the hills, as far as possible from towns and villages, and derive great enjoyment from their proximity to the mountains. In our own day the countryside of Snowdonia has become one of the most treasured and rigorously protected areas in the British Isles, and no-one who visits North Wales is in any doubt as to its overwhelming natural beauty. But no modern visitor to Ardudwy can fail to notice that many changes have taken place in the last two hundred years. When travelling along the main roads the evidence of recent construction confronts the eye at every turning. With happiness if one descends tired and hungry from the high pass above Dinas Mawddwy after a long drive, and spots the Little Chef just outside Dolgellau. With disquiet if one takes the trouble to visit a small lake above Llandecwyn, praised by many of the early tourists for its beauty, and finds that it has been bisected by electricity pylons and power lines.

If the landscape has been altered since the days of the early tourists, then attitudes towards it have also changed. The transition from the fear and loathing exemplified in Torbuck's writings, to our own veneration of what we now describe as unspoiled countryside, took place during the period covered by this book and largely as a result of the journals of the early tourists.

A tour which is typical of those undertaken two-hundred years ago is outlined by the Reverend William Bingley in the preface to his two volume *Excursions in North Wales* published in 1800.

In the summer of the year 1798 I was first introduced, from various accounts that had reached me respecting the grandeur of the mountain scenery of North Wales, to appropriate three months to a ramble through all its most interesting parts. I accordingly set out from Cambridge (where I was then resident) soon after the commencement of the long vacation, and proceeded, in the cross country coaches, immediately to Chester. From Chester I skirted the North coast of Wales, along the great Irish road, through St. Asaph and Conway, to Bangor. At Caernarvon I remained for a considerable time, making excursions in all directions among the mountains, and through the principal parts of the island of Anglesey. When I had examined all the places that I could learn were worth notice, I continued my route entirely round the country, visiting in my course Harlech, Barmouth, Dolgelly, Machynlleth, Llanidloes, Newtown, Montgomery, Welsh Pool, Oswestry, Wrexham, and Mold. From Mold I crossed over (towards the interior) to Ruthin, and proceeded through Llangollen, Corwen, and Bala, to Shrewsbury, whence, in the month of September, I returned to Cambridge.

Not satisfied with this single journey, I returned into North Wales, in the year 1801, and resided there four months more; during June, July, August, and September. In this latter excursion my time was chiefly occupied with examining the counties of Caernarvon and Merioneth, and the island of Angelesey, visiting again, in these counties, all the places that I had before seen, ascending most of the principal mountains, and searching around for other new and interesting objects . . .

The traveller of taste (in search of grand and stupendous scenery,) the naturalist, and the antiquary, have all, in this romantic country, full scope for their respective pursuits.

My mode of travel was principally as a pedestrian, but sometimes I took horses, and at other times proceeded in carriages, as I found it convenient. A traveller on foot, if in health and spirits, has, in my opinion, many advantages over all others: of these the most essential is that complete independence of every thing but his own exertions, which will enable him, without difficulty to visit and examine various places that are altogether inaccessible to persons either in carriages or on horseback.

The beginning of tourism in Wales can be dated accurately to the closing decades of the eighteenth century, when a number of books written by visitors were published. Of course these were not the first people to travel through the Principality and record their impressions, there had been many others spanning the whole era of recorded history. What made their writings important was that they were travelling for pleasure and out of curiosity to see what, at that time, was a little known region of Britain. Their publications were usually written in the form of journals or letters. They were not simply intended as reminiscences; they also offered guidance and encouragement to others wishing to make similar journeys. Most of the authors were members of the newly emerging middle classes who had the leisure, the means and the curiosity to travel. Although by this time making a 'Grand Tour' of the continent was well established as a fashionable prelude to a life of leisure, the concept of travelling solely for pleasure was still relatively new. If the word 'tourist' only became current in the 1780s it is also significant that the word 'travel' is derived from 'travail' meaning 'laborious effort'. A long journey could still be perilous and

ITINERARY.

		Miles.	
Monday, Aug. 14*th,*	From Bath to the New-Passage	24	
1797.	Across the Severn ············	3	
	Caerwent·························	3	
	Usk ······························	9—	39
Tuesday, 15*th.*	Abergavenny ·················	11	
	Crickhowel ·····················	6	
	Brecon ·······················	13—	30
Wednesday, 16*th.*	Bualt ··························	15	
	Rhaiddar ····················	17—	32
Thursday, 17*th.*	Pentre ·························	15	
	Hafôd ·························	2	
	Devil's-Bridge including Ha-		
	fôd grounds ················	4—	21
Friday, 18*th.*	Machynllyth over the moun-		
	tains ······················	20—	20
Saturday, 19*th.*	Talyllyn ······················	8	
	Dolgelly over Cader-Idris	16—	24
Sunday, 20*th.*	Dol-y-Myllyn fall ············	6	
	Cayne and Mouddach fall	4	
	Tan-y-Bwlch ················	10	
	Bethgelert ····················	8—	28
Monday, 21*st.*	Round and over Snowdon to		
	Dolbadern Castle ········	17	
	Caernarvon ····················	8—	25
Tuesday, 22*d.*	Bangor ·······················	9	
	Conway ······················	15	
	Round Caernarvon ············	$1\frac{1}{2}$--$25\frac{1}{2}$	
Wednesday, 23*d.*	Llanrwst ······················	12	
	Capel Voelas ·················	10	
	Cernioge ·····················	2	
	Round Conway ···············	$1\frac{1}{2}$--$25\frac{1}{2}$	
		270	

From Richard Warner's *Walk Through Wales* published in 1798.

(By permission of Coleg Harlech Library)

would certainly require stamina. Inns were uncomfortable places, to be used through necessity rather than for pleasure and, although improvements were rapidly being made in the road network, these did not extend to the remoter regions of the country. Until the second half of the eighteenth century people travelled out of necessity, to carry on trade or diplomacy, to find employment or seek a cure for some ailment.

When the first tourists came to Ardudwy in the 1790s they saw the same landscape which we see today. The mountains have not moved, the rivers follow very much the same courses in the valleys and, although the sea level may have changed slightly, the coast is still in roughly the same place as it was then. The changes which have taken place are ones of detail only. The building of new houses in the countryside, the vast improvement in the roads, the coming of the railways and the concentration of a larger population in the few towns are only significant close at hand. From the mountain tops they are barely noticeable, mere surface effects dwarfed by the vastness of their surroundings. What distinguishes the impressions of the early tourists from those of the present day visitor is not what they saw, but the way in which they saw it. By this I do not mean that they walked or rode along rough tracks and paths, when we drive on well surfaced roads, but that they had a fundamentally different perception of the countryside around them. Places which today are revered as 'beauty spots', as much for their freedom from the influence of man as for any aesthetic merit which they may have, were often described by our forefathers as gloomy, oppressive or desolate. Remoteness held no charm for them and they came to this area not because of its isolation but in spite of the inconvenience which this caused them.

Henry Penruddocke Wyndham published his *Gentleman's Tour Through Monmouthshire and Wales* in 1775. This was based on his travels during June and July 1774, and was clearly intended to encourage others to take an interest in Wales. The preface has a slightly evangelistic ring to it.

> The author of the following concise tour has no other view in the publication of it, than a desire of inducing his countrymen to consider Wales as an object worthy of attention.
>
> The romantic beauties of nature are so singular and extravagant in the principality, particularly in the counties of Merioneth and Caernarvon, that they are scarcely to be conceived by those who have confined their curiosity to the other parts of Great Britain
>
> Notwithstanding this, the Welch Tour has hitherto been strangely neglected; for while the English roads are crowded with travelling parties of pleasure, the Welch are so rarely visited, that the author did not meet with a single party during his six weeks journey through Wales.
>
> We must account for this from the general prejudice which prevails, that the Welch roads are impracticable, the inns intolerable, and the people insolent and brutish.
>
> The writer of these sheets is happy that he is enabled to remove such discouraging difficulties, and assure the reader, that in the low, level countries, the turnpikes are excellent; and that the mountainous roads are, in most parts, as good as the nature of the country will admit of; that the inns, with a few exceptions, are comfortable, and that the people are universally civil and obliging.

His opinion of the state of the roads in upland areas was perhaps diplomatic rather than truthful; later writers express strong views on their roughness and inadequacy. Even when they were not, the eighteenth century traveller was faced with another serious problem. Compared to modern road atlases the maps then available were little better than sketch plans. Until 1794-5, when John Evans published a new, far more detailed set of maps of North Wales, tours seemed to have been planned on the basis of rumour and guess-work.

There were several factors which led to the increasing popularity of Wales as a tourist destination, and one of them, the economic and social changes known collectively as the Industrial Revolution, also brought about a change in the visitors' attitude to remote countryside. This in turn allowed later generations of tourists to appreciate the roughest aspects of the Welsh landscape in a way that would have been unusual even in the 1790s.

If the industrial revolution provided the wealth and leisure for the middle-class to travel, it also led to improvements in travelling conditions. Better roads to the new industrial centres on the borders of Wales made access a little easier, and during the early years of the nineteenth century the Turnpike Trusts began to build new roads in even the remoter parts of Wales, as new markets for raw materials and manufactured goods developed. However until well into the nineteenth century travel in North Wales was still a challenging business.

One feature of the Welsh landscape which the early tourists were prepared to tolerate discomfort to admire was the ubiquitous waterfall. Their interest in these amounted almost to obsession. This was partly because waterfalls represented for them an important aesthetic fashion which was summed up by the term 'picturesque'. In the twentieth century this word has come to be associated with 'chocolate boxy' illustrations or with pictures depicting particularly neat and tidy subjects. In the late eighteenth century and early nineteenth century the meaning was far more complex, combining romanticism with the analysis of the components of a scene in terms of pictorial composition. Towards the end of the eighteenth century this preoccupation with the visual components of scenery became a fashionable cult. Essays were composed, philosophies expounded, whole books written, in attempting to analyse the aesthetic pleasures which viewing certain kinds of landscape can bring. There is no doubt that the early tourists took the viewing and visual analysis of waterfalls extremely seriously. Their accounts are studded with opinions on the relative merits of various falls, their searches for local information which might lead them to one as yet 'undiscovered', and discussions of the best view point from which to admire them. They seem to have considered that they embodied all the essential characteristics of natural beauty, and there was considerable competition to produce the most telling account of their visits to them. Thomas Love Peacock, a man not renowned for being energetic, even sacrificed a night's sleep in order to view one by moonlight and consider the effects this had on the scene. Waterfalls could almost be described as aesthetic laboratories. We will be returning to this cult of the picturesque in the chapter dealing with the Mawddach Estuary.

When describing a visit to Goredale in the Lake District in 1793, John Byng speaks with the confidence of an expert.

I think that I may now say that I have seen the principle waterfalls of the north: not that any inspection can exceed the three beautiful waterfalls that are near together, and at a short distance from Dolgelly, in North Wales, which are buried in deep woods; and in this respect differ from the northern cataracts: a view of these occupied one of the most luxurious days of my life.

Even the rather sober Mr. Bingley was infected with enthusiasm. When nearing Harlech at the end of a punishing day on foot in the Rhinog mountains during the late 1790s he recalls;

..... I heard, from the side of a hill, on which we were walking, the falling of water, in a wood, on the other side of the valley, and apparently about half a mile from us; and I could, though the distance was so great, plainly perceive a silver line amongst the trees, formed by the waters rushing down a precipice. I enquired of the guide respecting it, and he informed me, that it was a fall of no great height, or beauty, and he was not acquainted with it's name, if it had any. My walk of this day had been long and laborious, and I was almost fainting from want of refreshment, so that I was under the necessity of taking his word for it, otherwise I should have crossed the vale to examine it, for I am much inclined to suppose, that it must have been a cataract of very considerable height.

This was somewhere close to Gwern Einion Farm, and nowhere on that hillside is there a sufficient body of water to supply a notable waterfall. Bingley tells us that the weather had been very bad that day, and after heavy rain nearly every mountain stream can look spectacular for an hour or two. But at this time waterfalls were a potent icon for the imaginative travel writer, and the merest rumour of an as yet 'undiscovered' waterfall

Rhaeadr Ddu near Maentwrog

could tempt authors into making errors. By 1808 George Nicholson, in his very comprehensive *Cambrian Traveller's Guide*, not only identifies the fall as a sight not to be missed but also names it, apparently with no more evidence of its existence than Bingley's casual reference.

Of course it was not waterfalls alone that made Wales an increasingly popular choice for the early tourists; these could also be viewed on the continent as part of the already well established Grand Tour. But in 1789 the French Revolution initiated an upheaval which was to affect most of Europe, and the wars which followed created difficulties for those wishing to travel abroad. Attention was focused on lesser known areas of the British Isles and particularly on Wales, the Lake District and Scotland. Many of the authors who wrote about Wales also visited one or more of these regions, indeed many had already made the Grand Tour before turning their attention to exploring their own country. Today, when it is possible for the holiday-maker on a package tour to travel almost anywhere in the world without really experiencing a change of environment other than that of climate (and even then only when they venture outside) it is hard to appreciate just how foreign Wales must have seemed to an eighteenth century Englishman. The language, the culture, the manners, the way of life, as well as the landscape were all very different from anything they would have experienced at home, and to them Wales would seem little less strange than one of the Alpine regions of Europe. The early tourists reacted in various ways to this stimulus. Some took a lively and inquisitive interest in their surroundings while others simply used their novelty as a vehicle to poke fun at anything with which they were unfamiliar. In this they were little different from modern tourists.

Many were attracted to Wales by the opportunity to dabble in science. As you will see from the biographical section at the back of this book, many of the authors were professional men who had been educated at university. Some were lawyers, clerics or businessmen who merely had scientific interests, but for others science was a career, and there were still discoveries to be made in this little known region. Their interests ranged through geology, botany, mineralogy and archaeology, but the more general terms antiquary and naturalist would be appropriate for many of them. Unfortunately the study of anthropology was too new to be significant in their writings, although Joseph Cradock, in his *Account of Some of the Most Romantic Parts of North Wales published* in 1777, did venture some remarks on the origin of the Welsh people.

> The origin of every nation is necessarily obscure, and always lost in a pretended antiquity. On the authority of Bochat we may trace the Welsh from Japhet, the son of Noah; according to others, from Trojans and Phoenicians, who were the offspring of Gods; and one writer I think has asserted that a True Briton is a compound of all nations under heaven. That Britain however was peopled from Gaul 1000 years before Christ, appears very probable.

The belief that the Welsh are the primitive remnants of the Ancient Britons, driven into the extremities of the country by the invading Saxons was general, and some chose to use the term as a form of abuse. Mr. Torbuck certainly did so, and as we shall see, he also held the kind of opinions about the Welsh which Wyndham was concerned about in the preface to his *Gentlemen's Tour.* Most of the early tourists were drawn from an exalted social background in which such sentiments would have been considered quite natural. If Wyndham, who was a wealthy landowner, praised the Welsh in the preface to his book, there is ample evidence in the body of the text which indicates a demanding and not always generous nature.

Until the early years of the eighteenth century the main means of accumulating wealth was from the land. For the great majority of the population prosperity, or miserable poverty, depended on the productivity of the land on which they lived. For those who owned little or no land, or inhabited areas which were difficult to farm, life was extremely bleak. The miseries of the poor were all too apparent in an age when there was little provision for assisting those who were suffering hardship. It is not surprising that the earliest tourists had difficulty in seeing the dramatic landscape of Ardudwy, which lay above the cultivated lowlands, with the objectivity necessary to appreciate its beauty. To them it was barren, and barrenness was too closely associated with starvation to allow them to view it as anything other than depressing and melancholy.

A passage from one of Lord George Lyttleton's letters to Mr Bower, describing his visit to Wales in 1756, illustrates this attitude. The lake which he refers to is Llyn Tegid at Bala.

> After we left the banks of the lake, where we had an agreeable day, we got again into the desert; but less horrid than I have already described, the vale being more fertile, and feeding more cattle. Nothing remarkable occurred in our ride, until we came to Festiniog.

If industrialisation has now divorced us from our natural environment, and to some extent allowed us to dominate it, then it has also given us the security to appreciate aspects of our surroundings which it would have been impossible to see objectively two hundred or more years ago. The modern tourist is likely to derive great pleasure from the scenery between Bala and Ffestiniog.

There were other obstacles to be overcome before tourists could turn their attention from the Continent to Wales. William Hutton bravely addresses one of them in the preface to his *Remarks on North Wales* published in 1803, but ends up being rather condescending.

> In former years, the English rarely entered Wales but to destroy it. Her sovereign mountains, beautiful valleys, and surprising cascades, instead of being admired, were tinged with blood. Nor was the eye of curious fascination with her wonders till within the last fifty years. The improvement of her roads, and particularly the daily communication between England and Ireland, brought her into notice.

The English traveller, at length, ventured to climb her precipices, descend her glens, and admire her curiosities, and now the vast influx of annual visitants enrich her with their wealth. If the fathers oppressed her, their children support her.

Though the world is frequently favoured with WELSH TOURS; yet the historical knowledge is still in it's infancy....... If much is said, much remains.

I follow the footsteps of no author, but make those remarks only which fell under my own eye, in travelling sixteen times, in various directions, through that principality.

In view of the history of Anglo-Welsh relations it is perhaps surprising that the tourists and their hosts managed to get on so well together, and this probably had less to do with the sensitivity of the former than with the tolerance and forbearance of the latter. In our own time, ill feeling between the English and the Welsh is probably more apparent than it was two hundred years ago, but this is the result of demographic changes, not bloody conflict. Though the problem is focused on the use of the Welsh language, this is a symptom of far more deeply seated cultural differences; the tension which these cause is one of the sadder aspects of life in Wales today.

Most tourists have trouble with the language of the countries they visit, but it is difficult to excuse the disdain with which the early tourists treated Welsh. At a time when a large part of the population had no reason to speak any other tongue but their own, these visitors seem to have considered the inhabitants' inability to speak English as a sign of primitive ignorance. They were unaware that this beautiful and expressive language is far more than a relic of former isolation. It was, and still is, the key to a culture and to a way of life which is uniquely Welsh and which can only find expression through that language. Indeed it is still easy to find visitors who see its use as wilful obtuseness on the part of local people.

Dr Mavor recalls a visit to a bookshop in Dolgellau in *A Tour Round Wales* which he published anonymously in 1806. His sensitivity is a rare exception.

> Called on Mr. Williams, the bookseller, stationer, and printer of the place, and purchased a Welsh grammar and vocabulary: he was pleased to find that I could pronounce some of the Welsh words better than the generality of strangers; and this compliment I had received from others. Except the 'll' there are few words but what an Englishman might easily master: That seems to bid defiance to all but native organs.
>
> Some years ago, I was informed, not a person in Dolgellau could tell an English traveller the road he was to take; but now our language is commonly understood, and spoken by considerable numbers: ....

The early tourists make little reference to the language other than to comment on the problems caused them by the inability of the locals to speak English, and occasionally providing notes on the pronunciation of place names. By 1847 John Hicklin felt that it was worthwhile including some simple phrases in his *Illustrated Hand-Book of North Wales.* These were particularly chosen for their usefulness when staying at rural inns, and some of them are particularly revealing because of the subjects chosen.

The English traveller will find no inconvenience from his ignorance of the Welsh language at the principal inns on the main roads. But, at others, where he might find it necessary to make a halt, and on his peregrinations from one place to another, especially in the interior of the country, he will often experience some difficulty in having his enquiries understood, or understanding the answers of the natives. In order to render him some assistance in this emergency, we subjoin a few queries and directions, such as it is natural to suppose the traveller will have frequent occasion to be solved, or to give, on his travels and at his inn.

Will you hang my top-coat by the fire to dry?
Rhowch fy nghob wrth y tan i sychu.
I wish to take a bed here to-night.
Dymunwn gael gwely yma heno.
Let it be aired.
Gochelwch ei fod yn damp.
Damp beds are very dangerous.
Mae gwelyau damp yn bur beryglus.
Bring me a pint of sherry wine.
Dygwch i mi beint o win gwyn.
Let my boots be cleaned.
Perwch lanhau fy mwtias.
I want my breakfast.
Mae arnaf eisieu fy moreufwyd.
Is there not a waterfall in the neighbourhood?
Onid oes yma raiadr yn y gymmydogaeth hon?

The author does not feel that it is necessary to include the Welsh for 'please', 'thank you' or any kind of greeting. The phrases chosen are mainly those which might be used by a humble landlord when receiving an illustrious traveller, who would not otherwise appreciate the degree of deference which was being shown to him. The failure to use these simple but very important phrases could only give offence among a people whose language is particularly expressive in matters of hospitality and courtesy.

In spite of these problems, from 1795 onwards the publication of tours in Wales became fashionable, and there was a large and growing market for this kind of travel book. Not surprisingly, those who were leaders in the field guarded their position jealously. In this excerpt from Joseph Cradock's pioneering *Account of Some of the Most Romantic Parts of North Wales*, published in 1777, he may be referring to tourists on the continent, but his remarks apply equally well to Welsh tours.

> As everyone now who has traversed a steep mountain, or crossed a small channel, must write his tour, it would be almost unpardonable in me to be totally silent, who have visited the most uninhabited regions of North Wales — who have seen lakes, rivers, seas, rocks, and precipices, at unmeasurable distances, and who from observation and experience can inform the world, that high hills are difficult of access, and the tops of them generally very cold.

Such irony is understandable, but even if he may have considered a tour at home to be rather tame, his account of his travels is more entertaining than most.

By 1800 Welsh tours followed a well defined pattern, and though they contain much fascinating information, there is a degree of predictability about them. The majority of the authors enter Wales either from Chester or Shrewsbury and make a circular tour which invariably includes Aberglaslyn, Snowdon, all the main waterfalls, some castles, as well as an attempted ascent of Cadair Idris, which was thought by many at the time to be the second highest mountain in Wales. If the route which they followed seems to suggest a sheep-like lack of initiative it is also true that the state of the roads limited the opportunities for choice. In Ardudwy the early tourists only had two alternatives after entering the district, either at Dolgellau in the south or Tan-y-bwlch in the north. Those who were in a hurry could use the direct route between Dolgellau and Tan-y-bwlch, pausing to view the waterfalls around Ganllwyd on their way, and this provided a fairly easy day's journey which could be accomplished in the relative comfort of a carriage. Those who wished to cover the ground more thoroughly would follow the Mawddach Estuary to Barmouth and then travel up the coast either crossing the Traeth Bach and Traeth Mawr to reach Aberglaslyn or rejoining the main route at Maentwrog. This was a far more demanding option as we will see.

If the early tourists can be excused for following each other's routes, it is less easy to forgive them for copying from each other's books. This practice was common and they were quite happy to include their predecessor's descriptions of places they had not visited themselves, omitting any reference to the true author. This can make it difficult to distinguish between what is original and what is plagiarism. Similarities in the descriptions of other scenes cannot be explained by the coincidence of using the same adjectives. Though it is natural that they would be familiar with previously published works there seems to have been little respect for originality.

All, indeed, owe a debt to Thomas Pennant, who published his extremely detailed three volume *Tour in Wales* in 1778. His work is so well known, and his coverage of the area so thorough, that I have drawn sparingly on it, using less well known authors where possible. Anyone who knows his writings will recognise that those who followed him were familiar with this work. Nearly all the early tourists who visited Cwm Bychan use his description of the Lloyd families' farm and lineage, either verbatim or précied. In spite of the title of his book, he was a scientist with a European reputation who can hardly be regarded as a tourist.

By the early nineteenth century the 'Welsh Tour' had become sufficiently well established as a genre for Dr Mavor to find quite a selection at the bookshop in Dolgellau in 1805.

> At Mr Williams' I saw a pretty good collection of tours through Wales, but it seems that the natives are not much pleased with any of them. Tourists who intend to publish, as was justly observed, pick up at random and set down at a venture all they hear; some are indolent, some inattentive, some credulous, and some write only to amuse.

This did not prevent him from publishing his own tour (anonymously) the following year, and though it is certainly very amusing, it is not noticeably more profound than many others.

One other author, who can in no way be described as a tourist, deserves mention here, and he is the twelfth century cleric Giraldus Cambrensis also known as Gerald the Welshman. He travelled through Ardudwy when he accompanied Archbishop Baldwin on a recruiting trip for the Third Crusade in the year 1188, and his words speak as clearly to us across the ages as those of any of the early tourists.

Early next morning, Gruffyd, son of Cynan, came to meet us, Humbly and devoutly asking pardon for having so long delayed his attention to the Archbishop. On the same day, we ferried over the river Maw [the Mawddach near Barmouth], where Maelgwn, son of Rhys, who had attached himself to the Archbishop, as a companion to the kings court, discovered a ford near the sea. That night we lay at Llanfair, that is, the church of Saint Mary, in the province of Ardudwy.

This territory of Cynan, and particularly Meirionnydd, is the rudest and roughest in all Wales; the ridges of its mountains are very high and narrow, terminating in sharp peaks, and so irregularly jumbled together, that if the shepherds conversing or disputing with each other, from their summits, should agree to meet, they could hardly effect their purpose in the course of a whole day. The lances of this country are very long; for as South Wales excels in the use of the bow, so Gwynedd is distinguished in the use of the lance; in so much that an iron coat of mail will not resist the stroke of a lance thrown at a short distance. The next morning, Meredydd, the youngest son of Cynan, met us at the passage of the bridge, attended by his people, where several persons were signed with the cross; amongst whom was a fine young man of his sweet, and one of his intimate friends; Merydydd observing that the cloak, on which the cross was to be sewed, appeared to be of too thin and too common a texture, with a flood of tears, threw him down his own.

Even if his estimate of the time it might take two shepherds to meet in the mountains is rather fanciful, his remarks do at least tell us something about land use at that time, and in an area which even now we might consider to be still in its primaeval state.

They continued their journey northwards along the sands of Harlech Beach, and Giraldus adds this useful explanatory note although his recollection of the geography of the Meirionnydd coast is inaccurate.

Traeth, in the Welsh language, signifies a tract of sand flooded by the tide, and left bare when the sea ebbs. We had passed over before many noted rivers, the Dysynni, between the Maw and Traeth Mawr, and the Artro, between the Traeth Mawr and the Traeth Bychan.

It is over eight hundred years since Giraldus wrote these words, a span of time which is difficult to imagine. Yet he was travelling through a land where Christianity was already very old. The church of St. Tanwg, at Llandanwg, which lies less then a mile from his overnight resting place at Llanfair, had already existed for 600 years and is still in use today. Although Giraldus's enthusiasm often over-rules the facts, leading him to take terrible liberties with the truth, his lively memoirs bring to life the excitement of travelling in an age which is far more remote from our own than that of the early tourists. But a lapse of eight hundred years did little to improve the accuracy of travel-writing, and it is as well to remember this when reading eighteenth and nineteenth century descriptions of Ardudwy.

The writings of the early tourists would be described today as travel books rather than guidebooks; they were as suitable for the arm chair traveller as for those actually visiting Wales. Not until well into the nineteenth century, when the first trickle of wealthy tourists was augmented by a socially more broadly based flood of visitors, did more comprehensive guides containing time-tables, listings of accommodation and complete descriptions of all the features and activities in an area which might interest the holiday-maker become common. A forerunner of this type of travel writing was George Nicholson's *Cambrian Traveller's Guide* published in 1808, of which W. M. Condry says in his outstanding book on the Snowdonia National Park, the 'revised and corrected third edition of 1840 is, after a century and a quarter, still a really useful book to take with you round

CAMBRIAN MIRROR,

OR

A NEW TOURIST COMPANION

THROUGH

NORTH WALES;

COMPREHENDING

THE HISTORY AND DESCRIPTION

OF THE

TOWNS, VILLAGES, CASTLES, MANSIONS,
ABBEYS, CHURCHES, MOUNTAINS, VALLEYS, WATER-
FALLS, LAKES, CATARACTS, AND BRIDGES,

IN THAT

INTERESTING AND ROMANTIC COUNTRY;

TOGETHER WITH

VARIOUS ROUTES

TO THE MOST ATTRACTIVE PLACES, POINTING OUT THE
DIFFERENT OBJECTS WITHOUT THE LABOUR OF
INCESSANT REFERENCE;

AND A SKETCH OF THE HISTORY, CHARACTER, AND MAN-
NERS OF THE PEOPLE.

BY EDWARD PARRY.

SECOND EDITION,

WITH A NEW MAP, AND OTHER ENGRAVINGS.

LONDON:
Simpkin & Co., and H. Hughes.
Wm. Curry, jun., & Co., Dublin.   Edward Parry, Chester.

1846.

(By permission of Coleg Harlech Library)

Wales.'. Much of the material which Nicholson uses is drawn from the writings of the early tourists, duly named and acknowledged by the editor as such; many of them are quoted at length. Unfortunately Nicholson writes in the oratorical style which gives nineteenth century prose a bad name with many modern readers. This also applies to a few of the passages quoted in this book. Fortunately one quickly becomes accustomed to the style and one can experience the excitement of discovering Wales anew through these first hand descriptions.

Edward Parry, a Welshman, published his *Cambrian Mirror or New Companion Through North Wales* in 1843. A quotation from a review in the Liverpool Journal, which the author reproduces at the back of his book, heralds the mass marketing of North Wales with heavy emphasis on the romantic.

> Mr. Parry, the enterprising Chester publisher, whose patronymic is inseparably identified with the renown of the Principality in history and poetry, has just issued a most comprehensive, and at the same time compendious guide-book to all the remarkable sights or time-hallowed localities in "the land of mountain and of song." We think so well of this excellent little publication that we will bestow a copious notice upon it in our next [issue], as we think that we cannot render a more acceptable service to tourists at this period of the year and in this vicinity than by making them in some measure familiar with its varied and attractive contents.

Finally here is an extract from *The Book of North Wales* by C.F. Cliffe published shortly before the coming of the railways opened Ardudwy to mass tourism and began a process which, in some respects, altered its character for ever. The cars which it refers to are not, of course, motor vehicles but their horse drawn predecessors.

There are four modes of penetrating Wales, vis., by car, by coach, on horseback, or on foot. We have tried all, and are disposed to side with Sir Richard Colt Hoare, in favour of pony-back, although that plan has some disadvantages. Most persons either walk, or travel by car, according to circumstances; and it may be laid down as a cannon, that the more leisure and the fewer encumbrances you have, the more you will enjoy an excursion.

CARS

Every respectable inn possesses its 'inside' cars, which are designed to accommodate three or four persons, with a small quantity of luggage. If the bounds of moderation be exceeded, by which we mean the retention of anything not indispensably requisite, the party of four must take a pair of horses, and very often use very old-fashioned but roomy and comfortable vehicles. The usual charge for cars is 1s. per mile, but sometimes you can obtain them for 10d. [4p]; 1s.6d. [8p] per mile is the rate for a pair of horses. The post-boys expect 3d. [1p] per mile. This is a good plan of travelling for a small party, who have not a private carriage.

COACHES

are not numerous, and notices of almost all will be found in the body of our work. Changes are sometimes made by the proprietors, so that it is impossible to write with precision. The following enumeration, however, will be found useful. We begin with the eastern side, making a circuit.

Shrewsbury. The Aberystwyth mail leaves early every morning, passing through Welshpool, Machynlleth, and Mallwyd. There is also a summer coach, the Greyhound, to Aberystwyth, by Newtown and Llanbrynmair. A mail runs between Shrewsbury and Newtown daily; and an omnibus creeps three days a week from Newtown to Towyn.

Llangollen Road Station. There is a coach daily (except Sunday) at 11.35 to Dolgelley, Corwen, and Bala, on the arrival of the 10.40 train from Chester. It starts from Dolgelley at 8.45 A.M.— A summer coach traverses the great Holyhead road between Llangollen Road Station and Bangor.

Ruabon Station. A small coach leaves Rhuabon daily, at 6.45 A.M., for Corwen, Bala, Dolgelley and Barmouth. It starts from Barmouth daily at 10.45 A.M. for Rhuabon.

Rhyl Station. A coach to Ruthin, and omnibus to St. Asaph and Denbigh.

Bangor. Coaches or omnibuses to Caernavon; and in summer coaches to Llangollen Road.

Caernarvon. A mail daily to Pwllheli. Also one to Tan y Bwlch, through Beddgelert, and Tremadoc. Summer coaches daily (except Sunday) to or from Dolgelley, Machynlleth, and Aberystwyth. One of these coaches runs three days a week along the coast from Tan y Bwlch, passing Harlech and Barmouth on its way to Dolgelley; the other takes the shorter road to Dolgelley, by Trawsfynydd, and (Oakeley Arms) Tyn y Groes.

A HORSEBACK TOUR

A man who does not live near the borders of Wales can only conveniently accomplish this by buying a stout pony when he enters the country, and selling it (at a loss) when he leaves. The best plan for people who reside within a moderate distance, however, of the point at which they wish to begin a tour, is to ride a galloway which they have already tested. A pair of old-fashioned saddle-bags will afford room for all that it is necessary to take in the way of luggage. We once, in company with two others, who were pretty well mounted, accomplished a tour of the latter kind, of 470 miles [756 km] on horseback, and about 130 [209 km] on foot, (we halted sometimes for a day or two, at an interesting place, to rest our steeds, and to enable us to explore wilds) altogether about 600 miles [966 km], in 28 days, out of which we rested four Sundays. No charge is made for beds when you travel on horseback; if a charge be attempted, it should be resisted.

PEDESTRIAN TOURS

It seems a work of supererogation [exceeding what is required] to offer a word of advice to the vigorous and numerous class of explorers who annually take to the road with knapsack or fishing-basket on back, and staff in hand; yet we have known and heard of so many cases in which a Welsh tour has been entered upon either in an absurd costume, or without due provision for the proper protection of the outer man against wet weather or rough roads, that a few words of advice from an old campaigner may not be thrown away. Pedestrians ought to penetrate the wilds and nooks of the country, and be prepared to face soaking days. A really good pair of shoes is the best desideratum. Let the soles be thick and broad through-out, with copper sprigs, and double upper-leathers, of first-rate pliable materials. Most fishermen don't mind their feet wet; but we recommend them to have moderately-high ankle-boots on the above construction, to button easily, not lace. Pedestrians will find these boots not despisable. Such shoes or fishing-boots as we indicate cannot be got cheap, and they should be seasoned a little beforehand. It is hardly necessary to tell those who walk, to economise the weight they have to carry as much as possible: narrow blue-striped shirts are the most useful; and by all means wear the universal light "Jim Crow" hat. Do not commence a tour , as many do, in old fragile clothes. A shooting jacket is best, especially on account of its pockets. If you can carry out a plan of sending a carpet-bag a-head to certain points, you will reap comfort therefrom; and will be able to manage with a very light load of personal luggage. The majority, however, make up their minds to carry a regular knapsack. A strong, useful umbrella, capable of being converted into a walking stick, will be found anything but despisable by pedestrians, for the light repellent mackintosh, if worn for any length of time, exhausts, and you may be obliged to walk through heavy rain for many hours. We altogether denounce the use of Regent Street boots and thin shoes in this rough country; the first wet day, or the first bit of turbary [peatbog], will make decided converts to this opinion. This to lady carriage tourists also.

The readiest restorative for bruised feet is hot water, with salt in it; and tallow has been found a valuable healer by many foot-sore pedestrians.

Modern remedies may come in impressive packaging but, for the walker, the problem of sore feet is a perpetual one.

CHAPTER 2

DOLGELLAU
AND CADAIR IDRIS

At the end of the eighteenth century Wales was still a remote, and to many of those who arrived there from England, an intimidating destination. Though travelling for pleasure on the continent had already become an accepted activity among certain classes, the tourist's itineraries usually led from one major city to another along well established trade routes, with only occasional excursions into wilder parts to visit scenes which were already becoming famous for their beauty. Though their journeys took them to distant places they were not breaking new ground, but following in the footsteps of many who had gone before them. It is ironic that the opportunity to explore far less well frequented territory should be available on their doorstep, within two days journey of London. Wales represented a new challenge to the adventurous traveller in those days, and in many ways it still does.

For tourists coming from the south or the east it was only when they reached the town of Dolgellau that they came to grips with the type of Welsh landscape which was making the country famous; a fame which was later to change its economy and its way of life for ever. Up to this point they had journeyed through valleys enclosed by high hills, but now they were among real mountains with the sea lapping at their feet. This bustling town, snugly situated in the fertile valley of the Wnion, was their gateway to Ardudwy. Whether they were walking, riding or travelling by carriage, they would have passed through desolate country, on rough roads, before reaching the sheltered woods and meadows which surrounded the town. The sight of smoke rising from the distant chimneys of the houses nestling beneath the eastern ramparts of Cadair Idris must have raised their spirits. Sadly, most were disappointed when they arrived. Reading through their journals it is hard to find anyone who had more than a passing interest in the place, and many disliked it. Writing in 1798, the Reverend William Bingley's description in *A Tour Round North Wales* is typical of many.

Dolgelle [Dolgellau] is a market town of some consequence, seated in a wide and fertile vale, between the rivers Arran and Mawddach [sic], and surrounded on all sides with high, and in many parts wooded mountains. The streets are irregular, and the houses in general ill built. The church is a neat structure, having in it an ancient monument of Meiric Vychan, an ancestor of the present family of the Vaughans of Nanney [Nannau], near Dolgellau.

Here are considerable manufacturies of Welsh flannels, which, from the number of hands necessarily employed, makes the new town very populous (about 2000). The market for the goods is chiefly at Shrewsbury; but of late years so much has been bought upon the spot, that they have had occasion to send very little to a market at so great a distance.

The Golden Lion, called Plas Isa, the lower house, is the best inn the town affords, but I cannot say much in favour of it. The provisions were not much amiss, except the wine, which was bad, and the beds were intolerable.

The Golden Lion Hotel has been empty for some years although, at the time of writing, plans are once again being made to re-open it. Wandering round its exterior the very dilapidation which it has suffered makes it easier to appreciate how it looked to the early tourists. Peeling paint has softened the lines of the few modern additions, allowing them to blend with the chaos of dormers, chimneys and wings which have been built piece-meal in earlier years. From the Marian car-park the back of the building presents a venerable, if rather ramshackle appearance, one vast chimney rising from ground level having an Elizabethan look to it.

If, at the end of the eighteenth century, Dolgellau was a busy commercial centre which had grown into a disorganised maze of winding streets on the banks of the Wnion, it has now become an attractive market town and administrative centre. When Bingley wrote his description there were no particularly large or impressive buildings to provide a focal point other than the fine old bridge over the river. To us it may seem strange that quaintness made no impression on our forebears, but they lived in an age when such places were simply backward and unfashionable; enthusiasm for old world charm would come later. Their first concern when they arrived would have been to find comfortable accommodation, but this was not always possible as we will see. Even if they were successful in this respect the town itself was not particularly to their liking, and they stayed there only because it was a convenient base from which to explore other attractions in the area. The problem was that the very characteristics which make Dolgellau so attractive to the modern tourist were disagreeable to their predecessors, but the surrounding area was, and still is, of great interest; visitors were prepared to endure the discomforts of the town in order to enjoy these. After a long and difficult journey they had much to look forward to.

Stranger still, from our perspective, was the early tourists' enthusiasm for new buildings. The author of a guidebook compiled in the mid-nineteenth century mentioned that the town had been 'much improved' by some new houses built since his last visit. How often do tourists today say the same thing when they see new buildings in old towns? That the Victorians built in stone is undoubtedly significant; that we, in a different economic climate, cannot afford to do so is undeniable. The parts of Dolgellau which were rebuilt during the nineteenth century blend happily with the remnants of the older town in a way in which modern developments could never do. In recent years the town has acquired new county offices, a by-pass and a vast new car park. Even the course of the river has been altered by embankments to accommodate some of these improvements. All of these have been necessary to adapt the town to the changed circumstances of the late twentieth century, but looking across the river from the car-park by the seventeenth century bridge one sees a dramatic example of what happens when old meets new to-day.

Fortunately the centre of Dolgellau provides us with a splendid example of a Welsh town which has changed relatively little over the centuries. It is one of those rare places where it is a delight to wander aimlessly, and enjoy whatever curiosities each

A side street in Dolgellau

new turning brings. The streets are built to a human scale and not to those demanded by the motor car. If, as Bingley complains, they are irregular, they make a pleasant contrast to the linear correctness of modern urban planning.

The tomb of Meurig Fychan can still be found below one of the windows in the church, though he looks a little uncomfortable in his surroundings. These suggest that there is still an active and prosperous congregation here which is much concerned with neatness. Though the present building dates from 1716, there is a reference to a church at Dolgellau in the Norwich Taxatio of 1254. On a table in front of the pulpit, close to Meurig Fychan's tomb, a fine alabaster font from this older building is displayed; an example of the strength of form which can be expressed in a design which is derived from the characteristics of the material from which it is made, and the means by which it has been worked. One cannot help wondering what the earlier church, which originally held this monument to a long dead warrior and such a beautiful font, would have been like. Their simplicity is notably at variance with the rest of the church's interior.

Thomas Roscoe, who published his beautifully illustrated *Wanderings and Excursions in North Wales* in 1836, was unusual in that he arrived at Dolgellau by the northern route. Considering the hazards which attended even the simplest journey in this area at that time, it is remarkable that he chose to travel at night.

> Being impatient to reach Dolgelley, I determined on delaying my visit to Festiniog until my return, and left Tan y Bwlch late in the evening in an open chaise, and a little before midnight arrived at Trawsfynydd, about seven miles on the road. The situation of the village, environed by bleak and barren mountains, is peculiarly wild and lonely, and, wrapped in the silence of night, now appeared doubly striking. But, on entering the inn, whatever might be the aspect of external nature, I found the inhabitants to be a jolly, self-satisfied race, intent upon eating and drinking, and enjoying, in their way, whatever worldly advantages had fallen to their share. It was, in fact, the evening of a fair, and the village inn was crowded with peasantry of both sexes; and the men, as if resolved not to yield in social prowess, drank and smoked like so many burgomasters. On observing the entrance of a stranger, they rose, drank his health, and soon began to sing, with much cordiality and some taste, a number of Welsh airs, in honour — I was assured by the complacent host — of my arrival.

Though my stay at this place was extremely brief, it was long enough for my driver to chime in with the revellers — in fact he became rather tipsy; and, after having, with some difficulty, saved him from breaking his neck by falling headlong over the wheels, I was compelled to change places with him, and undertake myself the office of charioteer. 'Albeit unused to the whipping mood,' I was enabled by my novel situation, to enjoy so much of the landscape as could be seen by moon and by starlight.

All mountainous countries have by night a perfectly interesting and romantic aspect; the dusky eminences seeming vaster as they rise in the distance against the sky, the valleys and hollows, contemplated from roads running midway along the face of steep acclivities, presenting the appearance of unfathomable depth, and every cwm, ravine or rocky pass, near to or through which I rapidly moved, seemed infinitely more wild than when day exhibits every object in full relief.

Having passed, without stopping, through Llanelltyd, I arrived about two o'clock in the morning at Dolgelley. At such an hour there is, of course, not a creature stirring in a Welsh town, and this one being unilluminated was beyond expression silent and dismal. However it was not long before I roused the jolly landlord of the 'Angel,' and, having obtained admittance into his castle, retired to rest.

Mr. Roscoe must have rested well at the Angel, for the next morning he rose early to visit Nannau Park and returned to his inn by lunchtime. His landlord seems not to have been upset by being woken in the middle of the night, and although still suspicious, he was willing to be helpful.

On my return to Dolgelley after my mornings ramble, mine host of the Angel, who expected my arrival, welcomed me with an excellent dinner. But from the number of queries I made about the localities, I doubt not — from some of his John Bull kind remarks — that he thought me rather a suspicious character; which I dare say was further strengthened by my midnight introduction to him, and being an entire stranger to the district. However, he was very civil, and, after I had finished my refection, proposed being my guide round the town. I could not refuse so polite an offer, and presently sallied forth 'to see what was to be seen.'

Dolgelley is encircled by mountains, and seated on the river Wnion, here a broad, shallow stream, over which is a handsome bridge of seven arches. It has a neat church, containing some old monuments; and a commodious county-hall, in which is a portrait of Sir Robert Vaughan, by the President of the Royal Academy. The picture, however, was suspended in such a bad and even dark a situation, that its merits may be said to be altogether lost.

The Angel Inn was not the only hostelry in the town, there was also the Ship Tavern and, of course, the Golden Lion which seems to have had the best reputation during the nineteenth century. Earlier, the accommodation available in Dolgellau had been spectacularly bad, even by the undemanding standards of those days.

Mr Torbuck recorded his sarcastic and bad tempered reminiscences of a visit to Dolgellau in *A Collection of Welsh Travels and Memoirs of Wales*. Though little is known about his life, he seems to have been accompanying a judge on circuit in Meirionnydd in the 1730s, and from his writings it is clear that he was one of those metropolitan travellers who consider that anyone living outside London must have escaped the civilising influence of that capital city. In other words he was also extremely arrogant. Such people can still be met with in the Welsh countryside, particularly in summer, and they usually seem disappointed and uncomfortable. The novelty of experiencing someone else's environment, and the opportunity to take part in their way of life, is quite lost on them. What they really want is the amenities of a big city, but with a beautiful view; they measure new experiences against their own sophistication, and find them wanting. Torbuck was certainly unfortunate in his accommodation at Dolgellau, but his intolerance and boorishness shriek from every line, and one cannot help wondering if he might not have deserved his misfortune.

From thence we departed, after Dinner, for the Town of Dolgelthlie, in Merionethshire, where we kept our first Assizes, or (to speak in their Language) Great Sessions.

In our Passage, upon the Brow of a Mountain, we were met by the High-Sherrif, at the Head of the Gentry: They were such as would hardly have pass'd Muster for petty Constables here; but there it was Colonel such-a-one, and Justice such a one. They were mounted on little Keffels [stunted horses], about a Cubit and a half high, to which a Scotch Galway, or Irish Garron, Look'd like Buecephelus himself; but what they wanted in stature was abundantly suppli'd with the Length of Mane and tail, and a deep Channel between every Brace of Ribs.

When he eventually reached the town, Torbuck set out to seek respite at the inn, but a greater trial of his patience than being bored by the greetings of country-folk awaited him.

Surrounded by a vast Tribe of the bare-footed Regiment, we got at length, to our Lodgings; where I desired my Landlady to shew me a good Room: That shall you have, says she, Got knows : And such a one as Christ nor Saint David ever lodged in.

And in that she spoke nothing but Truth; for it was a Ground-Chamber, whose Walls looked as though they had catch'd Leprosy. They were plaistered with Mortar of twenty different Sorts of Colours; and at the Bed's-head was a Cranny, through which the Wind diluted with Force enough to blow off a Man's Night-cap.

No less than a whole Cart-load of monumental Timber was carv'd into my Bed-stead; and it was to be ascended by a Ladder of six or eight Steps; so that it was highly necessary for a Man to make his Will before he went into it, lest, if he had tumbled out in the

Night, he had awaken'd in another World the next Morning, as infallibly he must have done.

The Ticking was so obdurate, that it seemed to be quilted with Flint-stones instead of Feathers; and perfectly drew Inden-tures in my Flesh.

Upon the Teaster [beam], a whole Race of Welsh Spiders, descended, as I presume, from the great Cadwalader, hung in Clusters, ready to drop into my Mouth, if I slept with it open.

I had a Pair of Sheets laid on as course as any Nutmeg-grater; I wish, to my Comfort, I could have said they had been half as clean; for they look'd as dimsy a Complexion, as if they had scrubb'd half the Keffels, or Horses, in the Country with them. When I expressed my Dissatisfaction, and told my Landlady, I did, at least, depend upon the Civility of a Pair of clean Sheets, as being used to wear pretty good linen: She reply'd, Got knows, I need not be so nice; they had not been lain in but six or eight weeks; she took them fresh off her Husband's Bed. And then, you know, I had no Reason to complain.

Well —- in I got, but could no more sleep, than if I had been in Regulus's Barrel, or Little-ease; for I had a Regiment or two of Fleas immediately at free Quarter upon me; which prov'd such admirable Phlebotomists, that I hardly knew myself next Morning, when I came to consult the Looking -glass. And they may talk what they will of their black Cattle, I am sure I found some of a different Complexion next Morning; and, in a Weeks Time, I was grown so complete a Grazier, that I could have flock'd o'er a Tartar in the Country. My Judge lodg'd in somewhat a better Room overhead; and following him down Stairs one Day, I had the Luck to find an over-grown Louse of the first Magnitude, on his Scarlet Robes. I was first strongly tempted to lay violent Hands on it, for its Audacity; but at last resolved to let it alone; concluding it must needs, some Time or other, Fall into the Hands of Justice; as no doubt but it did, though unknown to me. ....

But this was not all; Misfortunes rarely come single; In the Middle of the Night (wanting the usual Fortifications of Lock and Bolt to my Chamber Door) in comes a great Sow, who, I suppose, had been tenant in Possession there before, and came to claim Re-entry. She was so very big, that I was horribly afraid that she would have pigg'd under my Bed; With this grunting Chamber-fellow I was oblig'd to pass over the Night, but never in my whole Life before pray'd either so heartily, or so often, Phosphore redde Diem.

If Mr. Torbuck made a good story out of his experiences in Wales, which would be told and retold over the port after legal dinners for the rest of his life, perhaps his landlady also entertained her friends with her own version of their encounter; of how she had told a disagreeable 'gentleman from London' who had complained about his room that his sheets had come from her husband's bed, and how she had then let the pig into his room in the middle of the night by way of revenge.

Although the town itself held few charms for the early tourists it was still of great importance as a centre from which they could make excursions. Sir Richard Colt Hoare, artist, scholar and traveller, is quoted in most of the journals and guide books published in the nineteenth century as saying that he;

> '..... knows of no place in the principality, whence so many pleasing and interesting excursions may be made; and were nature bears so rich, varied, and grand an aspect as at Dolgelle'.

This is a strong recommendation from a man of wide experience who had not only travelled extensively in Wales, but also on the continent. Born into a rich (and eventually noble) dynasty of bankers, he had resisted parental pressure to join the family firm. After the early death of his wife in 1785 he made a considerable career out of his artistic and archaeological interests. His travels had already taken him to Holland, Germany, Austria, France, Italy, Switzerland, Spain and some of the Mediterranean islands before he turned his attention to Wales and Ireland when the French Revolutionary Wars made further excursions to the continent inadvisable. As a scientist he turned to the most fundamental material he could find when he was planning his visit to Wales. He chose to follow in the footsteps of Giraldus Cambrensis, as recorded in his *Account of Archbishop Baldwin's Itinerary Through Wales in 1188*, and he subsequently produced an edition of this work with his own annotations and illustrations.

The main attractions around Dolgellau were Cymer Abbey, Nannau Park, the waterfalls around Ganllwyd and of course Cadair Idris. All these lay within easy travelling distance of the town and they provided enough variety to please most tastes. Thomas Roscoe, ever hurrying on, visited Cymer Abbey *en route* to his next destination.

My path now lay towards Barmouth, and I, therefore, left Dolgelly the next morning, by what is called the Old Road. I surmounted the steep hill, and branched off to the right, by a footpath across some meadows, turned up the old sycamore avenue, to visit the ruins of Kymmer Abbey, or Y Vanner, as it is known by the country people, lying in desolation by the side of the Mawddach, about a quarter mile above the bridge. Viewed in combination with the rich diversity of objects presenting themselves along the course of the stream, the approach to this time-worn monument of vanished ages has something sombre and impressive. Above, in the distance, towers the dark rock of Moel Orthrwm; below, several valleys, watered by the intermingling of several streams, their banks studded with pleasant homesteads; on one side appears the bridge, and on the other extends the flat ground on which stand the relics of the antique abbey. Only a portion of the church is now to be seen; the great hall or refectory, and a part of the Abbot's residence, have resigned their more costly and spiritual charge for the less dignified, but not less necessary, avocations of a farm-house, from which are seen the lofty peaks of Cader Idris towering into the clouds. The east side is in the best state of preservation, and through its close mantle of ivy may be perceived the small narrow windows peculiar to old religious edifices. I observed, also, some rather minute Gothic pillars and arches against the south wall, and an aperture, in which, probably, was preserved the holy water. The space of ground within the walls is more than usually circumscribed.

It is still possible to follow Roscoe's route from the centre of the town to the abbey, and this provides a pleasant thirty minute walk. Cross the bridge over the Wnion, turning left and then right into Fordd Pen y Cefn, which leads to the golf club. Pass to the right of the car park and take the path downhill behind Hengwrt, the ancient seat of one of the branches of the Vaughan family. Unfortunately sycamores are not particularly long lived trees and the avenue mentioned by Roscoe has long since disappeared. Turn right at the gate at the end of the path and follow the road for a short distance to reach the abbey.

If you are driving then you will find the abbey well signposted from the A470 between Dolgellau and Llanelltyd, with a pleasantly situated car park by the river just after you turn off the main road. A short walk will bring you to your destination, but do not be discouraged by what you see on the way. Though the abbey was surrounded by open countryside in Roscoe's day, it was also inundated by ivy and in a state of dilapidation. Now it is one of the triumphs of Cadw, the organisation which maintains historic monuments in Wales; sensitively landscaped and with recent developments close to the site effectively screened by cypresses. The moment you walk through the gate you experience that feeling of peace which is the special legacy of the medieval church builders. The Cistercians were an austere order, who attached great importance to finding remote and beautiful sites for their foundations, and this one is no exception. The spirit of these men, who were prepared to labour for more than one generation in order to create a building which was as near perfection as they were capable of making it, lives on in their work many hundreds of years after the completion of the abbey. The ivy has been cleared away and one can now see clearly the simple beauty of the stonework. The exalting shape of its Gothic arches is echoed by the summit of Cadair Idris peeping over the trees in the distance.

When the Reverend William Bingley visited the abbey in 1798 he gave a brief account of its history.

This abbey was founded about the year 1200 for the monks of the Cistercian order, from Cwm Hir in Radnorshire, by Meredith and Griffith, the sons of Cynan ap Owen Gwynedd, Prince of North Wales. This seems (says a Welsh writer) to have been a colony of monks, sent off by that monastery, as bees do when the hive is too full.

About thirty years after the supposed period of its foundation, Kemmer Abbey appears to have been in a flourishing state. At this time, when Henry III was marching against the Welsh, who had risen, under their prince, Llewelyn ap Iorwerth, and attacked the castle of Montgomery, one of the monks of Kemmer happened to be near, and was questioned as to the position and strength of the Welsh army. He considered it a duty to befriend his country, rather than assist the enemy, and therefore deceived them so much by his report of the state of the opposing forces, that Henry determined on an immediate attack. The Welsh, at the first onset, feigned a retreat to a neighbouring marsh. The English soldiers, encumbered as they were with their armour, plunged, without hesitation, after them; and as soon as the enemy saw that the greater part were in the marsh, and unable either to react offensively or to retreat, they returned upon them with so much fury, as, after a short conflict, to come off victorious. This deception enraged the king, and not long afterwards, as he passed the abbey with his army, he ordered the abbey to be set on fire and destroyed. All the offices were consumed, but the abbot saved the rest of the building by his entreaties to the king, and paying down 300 marks.

At the dissolution of the abbeys the revenues of Kemmer were estimated at betwixt 50l. and 60l. a year. The site remained in the crown till the reign of Queen Elizabeth, who, about the year 1578, granted it to Robert, Earl of Leicester.

According to modern historians the founder was Maredudd alone and the date was 1198, just ten years after Giraldus Cambrensis passed through Ardudwy.

Long after the Cistercians had ceased to exert their influence on the area a wave of religious revival rolled across Wales, and this brought to Ardudwy a man to whom the hardships of the eighteenth century roads became a way of life. John Wesley was not a tourist in the strict sense, but he was certainly a great traveller at a time when the discomfort this involved kept most people close to home. He is said to have covered over 250,000 miles on his preaching tours, always it seems, at break-neck speed. For 66 of his 88 years he kept a diary, and though this makes it clear that he was usually preoccupied with evangelism (the main object of his journeys), he still comments on the day to day events of his travels. Between 1749 and 1756 he passed through Dolgellau several times on his way to Caernarfon, and whereas the early tourists came in the traditional holiday months of June, July and August he gives us some idea of what travelling conditions could be like in winter.

Wednesday, 21st. March 1750.

An hour and a half before we came to Dolgellau the heavy rain began. We were on the brow of the hill so we took all that came, our horses being able to go but half a foot pace. But we had amends made us at our inn. John Lewis and all his house gladly joined with us in prayer, and all we spoke to appeared willing to hear and to receive the truth of love.

The Rhinog Mountains from the east

He spent the next day at Dolgellau before travelling on to Tan-y-bwlch on his way to the north coast, but the weather had not improved.

Friday, 23rd. March 1750.

Before we looked out we heard the roaring of the wind and the beating of the rain. We took horse at five. It rained incessantly all the time we rode. And when we came on the great mountain, four miles from the town (by which time I was wet from neck to waist) it was with great difficulty I could avoid being borne over my mare's neck, the wind being ready to carry us all away. Nevertheless about ten we came safe to Tan-y-Bwlch.

Six years later he encountered even worse conditions before he reached Dolgellau.

Tuesday, 23rd. March 1756

When we took horse there was nothing to be seen but a waste of white, the snow covering both hills and vales. As we could see no path, it was not without much difficulty as well as danger that we went on. But between seven and eight the sun broke out and the snow began to melt. So we thought that all our difficulty was over till, about nine, the snow fell faster than ever. In an hour it changed into hail which, as we rode over the mountains, drove violently in our faces. About twelve this turned into hard rain followed by an impetuous wind. However, we pushed on through all, and before sunset came to Dolgellau.

Here we found everything we wanted except sleep, of which we were deprived by a company of drunken, roaring sea-captains who kept possession of the room beneath us till between two and three in the morning, so that we did not take horse until after six. And then we could make no great speed, the frost being exceeding sharp and much ice on the road.

On each of these occasions this road would have taken him close to the waterfalls which later became famous attractions for visitors to Dolgellau, but of course he did not visit them. Some years were yet to pass before the writings of the early tourists were to bring these to the notice of the general public as important examples of the 'picturesque'. The Reverend John Evans makes it clear in 1798 that he was an experienced visitor to such places.

> The traveller here cannot resist the invitation to look at nature in her fantastic wilderness, as exhibited in the celebrated falls of Cayne and the Mawddach. The weather for several days had been prodigiously stormy, and consequently favourable to seeing them to their highest advantage. Whoever visits these scenes in the drought, that frequently accompanies the most pleasing time for travelling, will be totally disappointed; for several of these falls will have vanished; and the person by whose description the traveller has been allured to the spot, lie under the imputation of misrepresentation or of high colouring.

Holidays in the mountains have the great advantage of providing plenty to do and plenty to see, in good weather at least; but the weather in the mountains is seldom reliable. It is fortunate that there are a few activities which positively benefit from bad weather, even if the cost of enjoying them is a thorough soaking. A sluggish stream trickling over bare rocks can, within a few hours, become a thundering cascade which shakes the ground under your feet, and although those who visit them on a fine day may well be charmed, they are unlikely to be impressed.

This is how the Reverend Richard Warner describes his visit to the most easily accessible of the falls in 1797.

The first cataract to which our guide conducted us was Dol-y-Myllyn [Dolmelynllyn; often referred to as Rhaeadr Ddu], situated a little beyond the fifth mile-stone from Dolgelly, near the house of William Madox, Esq. Passing through a white gate to the left hand of the road, we approached the fall by a path which climbs a pretty steep acclivity, clothed with trees of various kinds, and sprinkled with numerous uncommon and curious plants. This ascent continues the better part of half a mile, when the fall opens itself to view. We first observed it from above. Here the water seems to throw itself down a perpendicular descent of full forty feet, in two principle sheets, and thro' some lateral gullies, into a hideous bed of black, disjointed rocks, through which it struggles for a few yards, and is then lost to the spectator in the surrounding woods. To obtain a view of its further progress we struck into a steep and intricate path, which led us to the foot of the cascade, where the scene became much more grand, beautiful, and extensive, than before. An additional fall of twenty-five feet now appears immediately in front; the first cataract, and the ragged channel into which it discharges itself, are seen to the left hand; and to the right, perpendicular rocks crowned with noble trees, which throw their broad arms over the glittering waters, and relieve with sober shade their dazzling splendour.

To find the waterfalls, follow the A470 north from Llanelltyd for about 4 miles, to Ganllwyd, where you will see a car park on your right. Walk back along the road for fifty yards and turn right through a gate (sign-post to Rhaeadr Ddu). A steep road follows the right bank of the Afon Gamlan which tumbles over countless minor falls through a beautiful oak wood. Continue up the hill for a quarter of a mile, then take a rough path which strikes off to the left, bringing you to the bridge below the main falls. Don't miss the inscribed slate tablet on the right bank, just above the bridge, which shows how seriously the early tourists took their water-falls. It bears a quotation from Thomas Gray's

'Ode to the Deity of the Grand Chartreuse' and the best view is from a point beside this stone.

Warner might have been forgiven for deciding that one waterfall was enough for the day. He was travelling on foot, and had just spent a most uncomfortable night in Dolgellau after a strenuous walk from Machynlleth, via the summit of Cadair Idris, the previous day. His destination for that night was the inn at Tan-y-bwlch and had he known what his reception there would be like, he might well have hurried on his way. An account of his experiences later in the day is given in Chapter 5, but meantime, oblivious of the disasters to come, he sets out on a major detour to visit the other waterfalls at the head of the deep valley opposite Dolmelynllyn.

An infinite variety of shrubs and trees planted by the hand of nature, but disposed with the justest taste and the happiest effect, complete the beauty of this fairy region; the trembling foliage of the aspen; the vivid berries of the mountain ash; and the melancholy shade of the pendent birch.

Our first object was the Pistyl-y-Cayne, or fall of the Cayne; in order to approach which we passed over a rude Alpine bridge, formed of the trunk of an oak, thrown from rock to rock, and hanging over a black torrent that roared many feet beneath it. We descended with some difficulty to the bottom of the fall. Here the effect is very august. A sheet of water is seen pouring down a declivity, nearly perpendicular, of two hundred feet; the view of it complete and full, uninterrupted by the adjoining woods, which, tho' they thickly mantle its sides, do not break by the intervention of their branches the continuity of the fall. After tumbling from the stupendous height, the agitated waters are received amongst rocks of a light dun colour, which their perpetual action has excavated into hollows of alarming profundity and various shapes, and through these they force their course, in order to unite themselves with the Mouddach, a few hundred yards from the spot on which we stood. Whilst we were contemplating this grand example of natures magnificence, the sun, which had hitherto veiled his head in the clouds, shone suddenly and full upon the descending sheet of water, and produced an appearance that conveyed no bad idea of an immense shower of diamonds falling from an eminence. After some time spent on this scene, we were led to the Pistyl-y-Mouddach, or the fall of the Mouddach, which it was necessary for us to view from beneath, as it is impractical to attain its summit. This cataract is of a character completely different from any we have before visited. Indeed we may extend this remark to all the particulars of Welsh scenery; each spot having, as it were, a character peculiar to itself, a circumstance which produces inexhaustible variety and constant sources of fresh entertainment to the admirer of nature. The Pistyl-y-Mouddach consists of three falls, submitted at one view to the eye. The first is a sheet of water about twenty feet wide, and nearly as many in height, which tumbles into a deep pool of thirty feet in diameter. From hence it glides over a second ledge, producing a fall of about thirty feet into another basin of large dimensions. Here contracting itself, it is discharged by a third fall of twenty feet into the largest and deepest pool, over the brim of which it soon boils into a rude congeries of rocky crags, and foams forward to its point of junction with the Cayne, ...

Although it is possible to take your car part of the way to these falls, there are advantages in parking at Ganllwyd and walking to them as the approach road is a very narrow one, running along the side of a gorge, and you will miss a good deal of fine scenery by driving. Follow the main road towards the end of the village where you will find a turning on your right which will take you down to a lovely old bridge over the river. As the road rises steadily through mixed conifer and oak woods, with the river tumbling through rocky clefts far below, you enter the deep valley of the Afon Mawddach. A mile further on there is a Forestry Commission car park on the right.

Oak trees predominate close to the river and you pass the picturesque relics of the gold mining industry which brought fame of another kind to this valley during the nineteenth century. The waterfalls are reached after another mile and are quite close together. Rhaeadr Mawddach appears first on your right, seen from a distance through the trees, but before you reach it you come to Pistyll-y-Cain, which is on your left just after crossing a bridge. This is no longer the ordeal which it seems to have been for Warner, and many of the other tourists, on whom the 'alpine bridge' across the gorge left a deep impression. Great care should be taken, however, when approaching the pool below the falls, particularly if you have children with you, as the path is narrow and can be treacherously slippery in wet weather.

You reach Rhaeadr Mawddach by returning to the main track for a further hundred yards and then branching right to the old mine buildings. Here you will find the rusted remains of a large pipe on your left. To obtain the best view of the falls, scramble down to the river-side beside this, but beware! The way is steep, and if the river is in flood a slip could be dangerous.

When you have enjoyed the falls for long enough it is worth continuing a little further up stream to a bridge from which you can see the river at its best. This is an excellent place to decide what to do next, not only because it is a place of great natural beauty, but also because it offers a number of attractive alternatives. If you wish to return by a slightly different route, then you can simply cross the bridge and follow the track on the other side of the river downstream as far as the footbridge by the Forestry Commission car park, where you can rejoin the road from Ganllwyd. If you would like to extend your walk slightly, you can take the steep path opposite the bridge, make a circuit of about a mile, and rejoin the main track just above Ferndale. You will see glimpses of Pistyll-y-Cain from above as you go up the hill, but presently you will enter a dense new conifer plantation. At a white post marked '30' turn left.

Even on a fine day this is a dismal place, made sadder by the sight of great oak trunks lying beside the path. These are the remains of the original woods which were felled to allow the planting of conifers. Such an act is made more hideous by the suspicion that much of this ground is too steep for the new plantings ever to be harvested economically. Oak is remarkable for its durability and it is probable that these relics of once beautiful woodland will bear sullen testament to this generation's stewardship of the countryside well into the next century. Presently you emerge onto a bulldozed track which is wide enough, and intrusive enough, to accommodate a twin lane trunk road. Continue left to another lovely old bridge where you can pause and look down along the river. This puts what you have just seen into the context of the past, providing a glimpse of how these woods once looked. Fortunately, in recent years the Forestry Commission has become more sensitive to the landscape in which they operate, but these plantations are not old. Time alone will not restore these scars and it would be encouraging to think that in the next ten years the Commission may take steps to repair the damage which has been caused to this valley with its justly famous waterfalls. All the early tourists comment on the beauty of these woods, and yet only a token fringe of them has been left along the river banks; in many places not even that. In an age when we are particularly concerned about 'vandalism' example must be important, and young people from the big cities use these tracks. We all have an inborn sense of beauty and harmony; this need not and cannot be taught. The vandalising of telephone boxes or the mindless destruction of a few dowdy trees planted on a bleak housing estate, as a gesture towards 'the environment', is quite insignificant by comparison with what has happened here.

Continue to a place where several tracks meet and bear left to reach a sign; 'To the Falls'. As you walk down the hill you will catch sight of fields and a farm on the other side of the valley; a last reminder of what has once been. A short steep path returns you to the river-side.

Most of the early tourists seem to have hired guides to show them the waterfalls, and this is not surprising at a time when the countryside was criss-crossed by foot-paths and no detailed maps were available. Nowadays there is little problem in finding one's way, and the only place near Dolgellau where the modern visitor may feel the need of a guide is on Cadair Idris in bad weather. From an early stage in the development of tourism, shepherding travellers to the summit of this fickle peak was an important cottage industry for the people of the town.

If the ascent of Cadair Idris was one of the main attractions for the tourist visiting Dolgellau it was also one which provided more than its fair share of disappointments. All too often their accounts tell of an optimistic departure on a fine morning, accompanied by a guide laden with all the provisions that they considered essential for such an undertaking, only to find that the clouds had reached the summit before them. Joseph Hucks terse recollection in *A Pedestrian Tour Through North Wales* is typical of those who made the ascent but were deprived of their just reward.

> Dolgelly is a large and dirty town: we took up our quarters at the Golden Lion, a good hospitable inn; and next morning, after breakfast, procured a guide to take us to the top of Cader Idris. We armed him with stores, and warlike preparations of all kinds (to wit) ham, fowls, bread, and cheese, and brandy, and began the ascent at nine in the morning, and continued to toil for three hours and a half before we reached the top. But, alas! expectation had again flattered us; for, though it was a most lovely day in the valleys, yet here we could not see fifty yards before us.

It is surprising how many parties seem to have pressed on in spite of atrocious conditions and a very real fear that they might not return. Mountaineering was in its infancy, and what is now, to us, no more than a rather energetic walk, was at the turn of the eighteenth century an adventure worthy of note. The matter of finding a reliable guide was taken very seriously.

G. J. Bennett records in his *Pedestrian Guide Through North Wales*, published in 1838, that:

> ..... as the tourist approaches the town before crossing the bridge which is flung over the Mawddach, a sign of some importance attracts his attention on the right: it runs thus:

R. PUGH
Guide General

To the Water falls, Cader Idris,
And all the curious scenery in
The vicinity of Dolgelly.

N.B. Licensed to let saddle horses.

This may have been the same R. Pugh who accompanied Francis Kilvert on his ascent of Cadair Idris nearly forty years later although it is more likely to have been his uncle. Longevity seems to have been a characteristic of these guides and Richard Fenton, who visited Dolgellau sometime in the early years of the nineteenth century mentions another, Robert Edwards, who was perhaps the most famous of them.

> Friday . . . 1808 Left Dolgellau and took the Road to the North of Cadair Idris to Ynisymangwyn, a party just before us going up the Mountain under the Convoy of Old Robert Edwards, the long accustomed Guide, who now near 90 ascends on average during the summer 3 times a week the summit of Cader, and when he comes down seems as active as a schoolboy, and often takes his rod and goes fishing. He was married, as appears by the register of the church, 64 years ago; so that it is most probable, from that circumstance and others confirming it, he is 90. He owns to 86; and of that age, he is certainly as surprising a Man as ever lived. He is a little man, and has been given to drinking all his lifetime when he could get it. For these 25 or 30 years he has had his support chiefly from the Revd. Mr. Nanney of Llwyn.

The old guide had evidently realised that humour can be an effective aid to advertising. Visitors to the town were handed this strange document.

Dr. Mavor, who visited the area in 1805, failed to reach the summit of Cadair Idris and for a very remarkable reason. He abandoned the ascent because it was too hot! However he did engage the services of Robert Edwards for this and other excursions, and has left an affectionate pen portrait of him.

> He is a little slender man, about five feet four inches in height, and not withstanding his very advanced age, hopped and skipped about the room with all the vivacity and agility of a school-boy. The manner in which he expresses himself is as droll as his appearance.

Lege, aspice Conductorem, et ride.

ROBERT EDWARDS

"Second son of the celebrated tanner, William Edwards, ap Grittith, ap Morgan, ap David, ap Owen, ap Llewellyn, ap Cadwaladar; great, great grandson of an ILLEGITIMATE daughter of an illustrious hero (no less famed for his irresistible prowess, when mildly approaching under the velvet standards of the lovely VENUS, than when sternly advancing with the terrible banners of the bloody MARS,) SIR RICE ap THOMAS!!! by Anne, alias Catherine, daughter of Howell, ap Jenkin, of Ynys-y-maengwyn; who was the thirteenth in descent from Cadwgan, a lineal descendant of Bleddyn ap Cynfyn, PRINCE OF POWYS. Since his NATIVITY full two and eighty times hath the sun rolled to his summer solstice; fifty years was he HOST of the HEN and CHICKENS ale-house, Pen-y-bont, twenty of which he was apparitor to the late right reverend Father in God, John, Lord Bishop of Bangor, and his predecessors: by chance made a glover, by genius a fly-dresser and angler. Is now by the ALL DIVINE assistance CONDUCTOR to, and over the most tremendous mountain CADER IDRIS, to the stupendous cataracts of CAIN and MOWDDACH, and to the enchanting cascades of DOL-Y-MELYNLLYN with all its beautiful romantic scenery; GUIDE-GENERAL, and MAGNIFICENT EXPOUNDER of all the natural and artificial curiosities of NORTH WALES; PROFESSOR of GRAND and BOMBASTIC lexicographical words; knight of the most anomalous, whimsical, (yet perhaps happy,) order of HAIR-BRAINED INEXPLICABLES."

He is rather too free in his use of the expletives of language, namely swearing; but I dare say the poor old creature only wishes to be laughed at, and to amuse his employers, which he never fails to do. He was dressed in a blue coat with yellow buttons, a pair of old boots, and a cocked hat and feather of enormous size. This last appendage or covering to his head, was assumed in consequence of his finding that we travelled in a carriage; for according to some regulations drawn up by a wag of the place, the grand military cocked hat is only to be worn when he attends peers, bishops, members of parliament, and other distinguished personages. His whole air was military though he had never been a soldier. He procured several little horses. Nothing could be so amusing as to see the guide, en militaire, with a long white rod in his hand, like another Merlin, setting out at a full canter from the door of the inn, on his Welsh pony, followed by a little cavalcade who could hardly keep their seats for laughter. During the excursion, finding that the inhabitants of a farm-house where Edwards had been accustomed to procure refreshments, were all gone to attend a mountain preacher, he consigned them immediately to the devils of Teneriffe, and could scarcely be restrained from forcing his way in at a window, in search of cwrw [beer] or bread and cheese. ..... During this excursion we were entertained with the conversation of our guide, who walked with the alertness of a boy. His account of the Jumpers [an extreme form of Methodism] in the neighbourhood was very free. " they are a set of fornicating sons of b———s," said he. It seems that they once attempted to exhibit their orgies in the town of Dolgelley, but the great mass of the inhabitants being uninfected with the fanaticism, some of the young men began to jump and howl with them, particularly with the female devotees, which put them completely out of countenance. Our guide talked much of 'curosity-men,' meaning naturalists; and enumerated among his followers some eminent names in science and literature; among the rest Sir Joseph Banks and the late Earl of Bristol. In the morning he came to take leave of us, and held out his hand to me with " God bless you! I hope we shall meet again!" Poor man! his age, his vivacity, were all calculated to inspire interest. May his

71

evening of life be yet long and serene; and may the angel of peace smile on him at his parting hour!'"

Even with the services of a guide it was not always possible to reach the summit of Cadair Idris, but the reason which Dr. Mavor gives for abandoning the ascent was most unusual. Mountains on the western seaboard, as they say, 'collect the weather,' and the writings of the early tourists abound with accounts of failed attempts and disappointments. Henry Skrine, who had obviously heard how magnificent the view from the summit is on a fine day, resorts to 'sour grapes.'

After our return to Dolgelly, a perpetual succession of heavy storms prevented our intended ascent of Cader Idris, and we were, after various attempts, obliged to relinquish the design, which, from the same cause, I have never since been able to execute. The same fate ever attended me at Snowdon and Plinlimmon; and such is the stormy atmosphere surrounding these great eminence, that I believe much leisure and patience might be exhausted in vain to accomplish this object, though sometimes an accidental sunshine may render it easy. After all there is less to be regretted in the prevention of these expeditions than an unpractised traveller may

Cadair Idris from Tŷ Nant

imagine, for the elevation is too great for any display of picturesque beauty, every distinction of the vales is lost in the general chaos of the surrounding mountains, and the disposition of their rugged tops, when viewed from above, is rather a curiosity than a pleasure. Add to this, the labour of the undertaking, with the chance of its failure by some changes above, which we from below can neither foresee, nor even discover when they happen; compute the dangers that may arise from storms, fogs, violent gusts of wind, and extreme cold, and you may easily imagine the undertaking not very eligible without a favourable opportunity.

Whatever the outcome of the ascent, a description of the view from the summit was essential, and here is one provided by Arthur Aikin in his *Journal of a Tour Through Wales* published in 1795. This is quoted by Thomas Roscoe who was one of the unfortunate ones who saw nothing.

We were now above all the eminences within a vast expanse, and as the clouds gradually cleared away, caught some grand views of the surrounding country. The huge rocks, which before we looked up to with astonishment, were now far below our feet, and many a small lake appeared in the valleys between them. To the north, Snowdon and its dependencies shut off the scene; on the west, we saw the whole curve of the bay of Cardigan, bounded at a great distance by the Carnarvon mountains, and nearer, dashing its white breakers against the rocky coast of Merioneth. The southern horizon was bounded by Plinlimon, the bay of Swansea, the channel, peeping through the opening of the Brecon mountains; and on the east, the eye glanced over the lake of Bala, the two Arrenig mountains, the two Arrans, and the long chain of Berwyn mountains, to the Breiddin hills on the confines of Shropshire. Dimly, in the distant horizon, was beheld the Wrekin, rising alone from the plane of Salop.

Roscoe has the courtesy to acknowledge Aikin's authorship, but many others included this passage in journals and guides without doing so.

For a full account of an ascent we turn to the Reverend Francis Kilvert who, during his tragically short life, compiled a diary which has secured for him an important place in the affections of those who have had the good fortune to read it. His great love of the Welsh countryside, particularly of the Wye Valley where he lived, and his meticulous observation of its moods and the life of its people, allowed him to record a way of life which has long since disappeared, and he does this in a way which is both unpretentious and totally convincing, for unlike so many of the writers we are dealing with, he had a real affection for and empathy with people who came from a very different background to his own. There is no hint of condescension in his descriptions of them, and his account of his day on Cadaor Idris is concerned almost as much with 'Old Pugh', his guide, as it is with the landscape or the excitement of an ascent made in very bad weather.

When he left the Golden Lion Hotel early on the morning of 13th. June 1871 his curiosity first took him to Woombwell's Menagerie which had parked its trailers nearby.

> Up at 5.30. Not a soul stirring in the house, the front door locked and the key gone. I got out by the garden door and through the wicket into the Marian Mawr. There was the caravan. The people were all asleep, but the lions were rustling and growling about their dens hungry for their breakfast. The caravans were full of strange noises of the different beasts. I knocked at the lions door and at the door of the osteriches, gnus, and antelopes, eliciting divers roars, groans, howls, hoots and grunts. In the town I met the guide, old Pugh, coming to meet me. He took me to his house and furnished me with an alpenstock while his good wife gave me some tea and bread and butter for I could get nothing at the inn.

My old guide comes of a family of Welsh harpers. His brother is now harper to (. . .) Sir Watkin's sister. Another brother who is dead won a silver harp at an Eisteddfod and was one of the best harpers in Wales. Pugh said that there was a harper at Corwen and another at Llangollen and he knew an old bard at Corwen. He told me that he had once been up Cader Idris 4 times in one day for a £10 wager against a reading party of 4 or 5 Cambridge men who declared he could not do it. On the last day of September a pouring wet day he did it and won the wager easily. He could have gone up the fifth time. A man on each side was posted on the top of the mountain and a man on each side at the bottom to see fair play and that Pugh did not ride up. It was stipulated that he should go up by the pony road and come down any way he liked. Coming down the first time he nearly came to trouble and was delayed 20 minutes in this way. He had noticed often when on the mountain that at a particular place his dog usually put up a fox and that the fox always disappeared down a cleft in the rocks. When walking for the wager he thought of this fox path and thought it would take him down quicker. Supposing that he could go where a fox went he slid down the narrow chasm and found that it led to the brink of a precipice. He could not go back and he was obliged to go on, so taking off his boots and slinging them round his neck he clambered down. He did not try that way again.

By this time we had come to a place where there was a lake by the roadside and in a boat on the lake were two men fishing. Leaving the road here we turned up a rough lane and crossing a little brook by a farm house were on the open mountain. As we sloped up the mountain side we had beautiful views of the Harlech mountains opposite, blue Cardigan Bay and dim Snowdon. The zig-zag path was steep in parts and a good wind blew over the mountain so that I had to sit down in a sheltered place and tie the band of my hat to my button-hole with the old guides neckerchief, for, said the old man, 'Many hats have been lost on this ridge'. We aimed for a great stone on top of the ridge. After this the climbing was not so severe. The old man came up very slowly. Soon after we passed the great stone we passed through a gateway the posts of which were large basaltic pillars. Here we saw a mountain standing close by waiting on Cader Idris. It was Plynlimmon. Here we passed round over the back of the mountain and began ascending the summit from the S. We came to a little round pool or rather hole full of water. The old man pulled a little tumbler out of his pocket rinsed it and gave me a glass of the clear bright water. It was delicious. Then he drank himself. He said the pool was the head water or spring of the Dysyni River. He had never known it dry in

the driest summers. We saw from the spring the winding gleam of the Dysyni wandering down a desolate valley to join the Dyfi, its sister stream.

About this time the wind changed and flew suddenly round into the S. The head of Idris, which had been cowled in cloud, had cleared for a while, but now an impenetrable dark cloud settled down upon it and the mist came creeping down the mountain. The sky looked black and threatened rain. Now there lay before us vast tracts and belts of stones lying so close together that no turf could be seen and no grass could grow between them. It was broken basalt, and large lengths of basalt, angled, and some hexagonal, lay about or jutted from the mountain side like enormous balks of timber and with an unknown length buried in the mountain. We passed quarries where great columns had been dug out to be drawn down the mountain on sledges. Cader Idris is the stoniest, dreariest, most desolate mountain I was ever on. We came now to the edge of a vast gulf or chasm or basin almost entirely surrounded by black precipices rising from the water of a black tarn which lay in the bottom of the basin. Here the guide showed me the place where Mr. Smith's body had been found. Then we stumbled and struggled on again over rough tracts and wildernesses of slate and basalt. The sun was shining on the hills below, but the mist crawled down and wrapped us as if in a shroud blotting out everything. The mists and clouds began to sweep past us in white thin ghostly sheets as if some great dread Presences and Powers were going past and we could only see the skirts of their white garments. The air grew damp and chill, the cloud broke on the mountain top and it began to rain. Now and then we could discern the black sharp peak which forms the summit looming large and dark through the cloud and rain and white wild driving mist, and it was hidden again. It is an awful place in a storm. I thought of Moses on Sinai.

The rain grew heavier. The old guide could not get on very fast and told me to go on alone to the top and shelter in the hut as I could not miss the path. So I went on up the last sharp peak looming black through the dark mist and cloud, by a winding path among the great rocks and wilderness of loose stone. For a few minutes I was alone on the top of the mountain. The thought struck me, suppose the old man should be seized by cramp in the stomach here, how in the world should I get him down or get down myself in the blinding mist? The cloud and mist and rain swept by and drove eddying round the peak. I could hear the old man clinking his iron-shod stick among the rocks and stones, as he came up the path, nearer and nearer, but till he got close to me I could not discern his white figure through the dense mist. 'This is the highest point of Cader Idris', he said, laying his hand upon a peak of wet living rock, 'not that,' looking with contempt at the great conical pile of stones built upon the peak by the sappers and miners during the Ordnance Survey. He said, 'The Captain of the surveying company had his tent pitched on the top of Cader Idris for three summer months and never left the place. He had 18 men to wait upon him, and how many clear days do you think he got in that time?' 'Twelve', I hazarded. 'Nine', he said.

He took me down to a rude 2-roomed hut built of huge stones by his father just under the shelter of the peak, and produced for my benefit a hard-boiled egg and some slices of bread and butter. Also he gave me a woollen comforter to wrap round my neck. Then he vanished, the mist drove in white sheets and shapes past the doorless doorway and past the windows from which the window frames had been removed and the wind whistled through the chinks in the rude walls of huge stones. A large flat block of stone in the middle of the room on which I sat formed the table. It is said that if anyone spends a night alone on the top of Cader Idris he will be found in the morning either dead or a madman or a poet gifted with the highest degree of inspiration. Hence Mrs. Heman's fine song 'A night upon Cader Idris'. The same thing is said of the top of Snowdon and of a great stone at the foot of Snowdon. Old Pugh says the fairies used to dance near the top of the mountain and he knows people who have seen them.

Presently I heard the old man clinking his stick among the rocks and coming round the hut. He came in and lighted his pipe and we prepared to go down by the 'Foxes' Path. And indeed it was a path fit only for foxes. After leading me a few steps he began to go over what seemed to me to be the edge of a precipice, depth unknown and hidden in the mist. The side of the mountain was frightfully steep here and required great care in going down. Suddenly the old man stopped at a beautiful little spring in the almost perpendicular bank, pulled out his tumbler and gave me a draught of the clear sparkling water, much colder than the water from the spring of Dysyni. About the spring the grass grew brilliant green and there was a long winding riband of bright green where the waters overflowing from the spring trickled down through the grass stems to feed the lake at which the foxes drink just below. Next we came to a broad belt of loose rocks lying close together which the guide cautioned me to beware of and not without reason saying they were as slippery as glass and that a sprained ankle was an awkward thing on the mountain. Down, down and out of the cloud into sunshine, all the hills below and valleys were bathed in glorious sunshine - a wonderful and dazzling sight. Above and hanging overhead the vast black precipices towered and loomed through the clouds, and fast as we went down the mist followed faster and presently all the lovely sunny landscape was shrouded in a white winding sheet of rain. The path was all loose shale and stone and so steep that planting our alpenstocks from behind and leaning back upon them Alpine fashion we glissaded with a general landslip, rush and rattle of shale and shingle down to the shore of the Foxes' Lake. The parsley fern grew in sheets of brilliant green among the grey shale and in the descent we passed the largest basaltic columns of all protruding from the mountain side. In the clefts and angles of the huge grey tower columns grew beautiful tufts and bunches of parsley fern. We passed another lake and after some rough scrambling walking over broken ground at the mountain foot we came back into the turnpike road at the lake that we had passed in the morning. As we entered Dolgelly the old man said, 'You're a splendid walker, Sir' a compliment which procured him a glass of brandy and water.

Francis Kilvert was justly proud of his ability as a walker. He must have been very fit for, as an impecunious country curate, his usual means of travelling round his mountainous and far flung parish was on foot. Those who wish to follow in Kilvert's footsteps up Cadair Idris will find brief notes on the route in the appendix on longer walks at the back of this book, but please heed the cautionary tale which accompanies them!

Before we leave the Dolgellau area here is a final outburst from Mr. Torbuck. He wakes on the morning after his discovery of the pig under his bed and tries to make the best preparations he can to face another day. Unfortunately he is still not in a frame of mind which is likely to improve Anglo-Welsh relations.

When I got up I called for a Basin of Water, to see if the liquid Element would contribute any thing towards meliorating my Looks. The Wench (to shew the Frankness of her Temper) brings no less than a Pailful, but so very dirty, that (excepting her own Face) I saw nothing likelier to turn a Man's stomach in a Morning Fasting. All that I shall say of my Towel is, That it was very correspondent to my Sheets.

I next sent out for a Barber (resolving to set the best Face upon Matters I could) and, in about half an Hour's Time, in comes a greasy Fellow, swift to shed innocent Blood, who, in a trice, from a portable Cupboard, call'd his Codpiece (a kind of jock strap), pulls out a Woollen Night-Cap that smelt very much of human Sweat and Candle-grease, and about two Ells of Towelling, of so coarse a Thread, that they might well have serv'd a zealous Catholick instead of a penitential Hair-Cloth.

After some fumbling, he pulls out a Thing he call'd a Razor, but both by the Looks and Effects, one might easily have mistaken it for a Chopping-knife; and with pure Strength of Hand, in a short time, he shaved me so clean, that not only the Hairs of my Face, but my very Skin was become invisible; for he left me not sufficient to make a Patch for an Æthiopian Lady of Pleasure;.......

Adversity often seems to inspire the best stories.

CHAPTER 3

THE MAWDDACH ESTUARY
AND BARMOUTH

The Mawddach estuary from Barmouth bridge

The early tourists were attracted to Dolgellau by waterfalls, the ruins of an ancient abbey and the opportunity of climbing a high mountain. Their interest in these had been inspired by a relatively new fashion in aesthetics which was summed up by the word 'picturesque'; the process of seeing landscape in terms of pictorial composition. Later in this chapter we will see how important this was in the early years of tourism in Wales, for it helped to break down inhibitions which had previously prevented visitors from enjoying the beauty of mountainous country. Until the end of the eighteenth century many travellers were as concerned with the discomfort and dangers of the roads as with their surroundings, but by the early years of the nineteenth century this wonderful estuary, enclosed by Cadair' Idris and the Rhinog mountains, had become a touchstone by which much of the landscape they subsequently

81

saw could be judged. Slowly the transition was made from regarding such scenery as merely threatening and depressing, to recognising its rare and powerful beauty. Fear of the wilderness was beginning to be replaced by an appreciation of wild scenery. This initiated a process which has resulted in the tourist trade penetrating the furthest corners of the British Isles, and in our own time has left few places on earth unvisited by those who travel for pleasure.

The Mawddach Estuary, between Dolgellau and Barmouth, played an important part in this process, but many of the early tourists passed it by. Those who chose to continue their journey northwards by way of the coast, rather than taking the more direct route to Snowdonia via Tan-y-bwlch and Aberglaslyn, now faced a difficult stretch of road which led through an area with less easily definable attractions. Though Barmouth was already developing a reputation as a seaside resort, and Harlech was famous for its castle, the area in which they lay was still considered by many to be a wilderness, so they chose the shortest route, which could be covered more quickly and in the comfort of a carriage. The rewards for those intrepid enough to follow the coast were in proportion to the risks which they faced.

By the time George Nicholson published his *Cambrian Directory* in 1808 the original line of the road had been altered and improved to some extent, leaving travellers free to concentrate on their surroundings.

The approach to Barmouth was formerly over a prodigious mountain, surmounted with great difficulty and passed with apprehension of destruction. The magistrates of the county, however, bent on improvement, agreed with an undertaker [contractor] to form a road out of the steep rocks jutting from the sea, and to guard it with a wall. The labour was astonishing, the price 2 guineas a yard. It is now a most charming road, exhibiting romantic boldness of scenery.

Even as early as 1798 the Reverend John Evans had been impressed by the scenery, but the improvements to the road nearly led to tragedy in his case.

The delight which we felt during this pleasing ride, was nearly terminated in a disastrous conclusion. The road near Barmouth is on the shelf of the rocky mountain, on which part of the town is built; which from the constant washing of the tide, had of late experienced considerable in-roads. A spirit of necessary improvement induced the commissioners to devise means to improve it. The most eligible plan was deemed, blowing up the rock. This was now executing by means of gunpowder; and the men were busily employed in the work. We had scarcely passed the spot before our horses started at an explosion unexpected by the workmen themselves; and a portion of rock gave way of many thousands of tons weight, which completely blocked up the road; fortunately no lives were lost; but had we been a few seconds later, we must have been inevitably crushed to atoms.

The line of the old road over the 'mountain' is still recognisable if you follow the path leading from the centre of Barmouth to the Panorama Walk, which is described later in this chapter, and seeing it makes the fears of past travellers very real. But if inadequate roads were a problem for the early tourists, then their improvement to accommodate faster transport has now impaired our ability to enjoy landscape while travelling.

The main road along the estuary can be busy at times, especially during the summer, and an interesting variation on the usual route via Llanelltyd can be followed by turning left off the Dolgellau by-pass towards Tywyn, and then right after about two miles and crossing the toll bridge at Penmaenpool. This is a peaceful spot where the old wooden bridge, the whitewashed

George III Hotel, and a gentle bend in the river overlooked by scots pines on a rocky promontory, combine to create a scene which lingers in the memory. Whichever way you choose to go, the Mawddach Estuary is constantly in sight, and there are few places where one is so conscious of the rapid changes in the appearance of the landscape caused by the effects of light and clouds. Our predecessors attached great importance to seeing the estuary at high tide, when they considered that it looked like a huge lake. But then they were concerned with the picturesque and this term, which we tend to use rather casually now to describe any scene which we find attractive, had a far more specific meaning for them.

As we have seen, the early tourists were drawn from the ranks of the 'chattering classes' of their day, so it was natural that their writings would reflect the latest intellectual fashions. Their attempts to see living landscape in the way in which a painter might represent it on canvas, and to judge their surroundings by the qualities which would be essential in the creation of a satisfying pictorial composition may seem quaint to us, but the effect this had on attitudes to the countryside is still important today. Their way of thinking provided a means of analysing what they saw in accordance with the aesthetic discipline which had been developed by artists over hundreds of years. Though few went as far as to carry a picture frame around with them through which to consider selected views, many did use the Claude Mirror* as a means of comparing well known scenes with etched images. The cult of the picturesque also led many of the tourists to include excruciatingly long, analytical descriptions of views in their journals.

---

*This device is particularly associated with the French painter of the same name, who used it to analyse tonal values of his subjects without the distraction of colour. A piece of glass was painted black on one side, and by looking at the reflections in this, the artist could see an image in which colour is suppressed but contrasts of tone and texture tell clearly. The effect is very subtle and not unlike that of an aquatint.

The Mawddach estuary embodied three of the elements which were considered essential to a picturesque landscape. These were mountains or rocks, trees and water. (The importance of these may also explain the tourists' fascination with waterfalls; ancient ruins such as castles and monasteries were also important components of the picturesque). But if considering landscape within a rigid framework of academic rules may seem alien to us today, it had at that time an importance that lay not in the formulation of rules and the writing of fashionable essays on the picturesque, but in the development from considering landscape as something which you travelled through, a hiatus between destinations, to something to be experienced and admired in its own right. The legacy of this change of attitude is with us today and still exerts a strong influence on the way in which we evaluate our surroundings. Once one begins to see the countryside primarily in terms of its visual beauty it may become more difficult to consider its function, and so the conflict of interest between those who live in rural areas and those who visit them for pleasure was born.

If the early tourists attached great importance to seeing the Mawddach Estuary at high tide, when it satisfied their ideal of completeness in composition, we no longer need any such contrivance to enjoy it for what it is at any state of the tide; an estuary with the slight air of untidiness which is one of the characteristics of such places. At low water, with the sandbanks exposed, it has a special beauty which is enhanced by the subtle variations in colour on the vast areas of sand, modulated by the intricate patterns left by the constantly shifting currents. The immense flatness of the estuary gives full value to the rounded foothills covered by native oak woods, and to the open crags of Cadair Idris rising high above.

The last two hundred years has left this vast inlet virtually unmarked, and the journey from Dolgellau to Barmouth still takes you through a landscape which is a constant source of delight. In 1796 Arthur Aikin did not go all the way to the coast, preferring to visit the waterfalls at Ganllwyd and then carry on to Tan-y-bwlch, but he was wise enough to make a detour in order to see the estuary.

We took leave of Dolgelle this morning, and proceeded about four miles down river to a forge; in our way we passed Llaneltid, a flourishing village, containing several good houses, beautifully situated on the River Mawddach, or Maw: it serves as a port to Dolgelle, and a good many small vessels are built here. We saw a stout brig of 168 tons on the stocks, and one of 210 tons had been launched a little before. These large vessels however are unable to get out of the shallow passage from Cardigan Bay to Barmouth harbour, except by taking advantage of the equinoctial tides. At this place also we met a large pleasure boat on wheels, proceeding slowly to Bala-pool, for the use of Sir W. W. Wynne. ..... Proceeding still [further] down the river, we just passed the forge, and came upon a prospect which, for beauty and picturesque effect, can scarcely be equalled. The wide estuary of the Mawddach was before us, filled by the tide, and enlivened here and there by a barge or pleasure boat; the banks on each side run out alternately in steep promontories, wooded to the water's edge, so as to completely hide the termination of the river, and cause it to resemble a broad and beautiful lake; while on the south from behind the banks rose abruptly the vast and craggy cliffs that surround, and almost conceal, the summit of Cader Idris.

Llanelltyd has changed since Mr Aikin passed by on that fine August morning. The estuary has silted up, to the extent that it would be difficult to launch anything much larger than a rowing boat here, and the impression which the tourist now gets of the village is dominated by a new road. However the description which he gives of the landscape is still valid today. The forge which he mentions cannot have been far from Borthwnog Hall, about two miles from Llanelltyd, which is now an excellent country house hotel with a well stocked art gallery specialising in paintings and prints by artists associated with this area. The view from the terrace in front of the house comes as a surprise, for trees hide this prospect from the road. In the foreground the river meanders through water meadows, the benign legacy of the silt which has restricted navigation since Aikin's visit, but otherwise things are very much as he describes them, with few reminders that this is the twentieth and not the eighteenth century.

Perhaps the most conspicuous man-made feature of the estuary, which would not have been seen by the early tourists, is the long wooden railway bridge spanning the Mawddach between Barmouth and Arthog. This carries the Cambrian Coast Line, providing an almost natural visual break between the enclosed scenery of wooded hills and sandbanks, and the vastness of the Irish Sea beyond. Until Dr. Beeching wielded his axe in the 1960s, ending rail services in so many rural areas, trains ran along the south side of the estuary to Dolgellau and beyond. When this line was built the disfigurement of the landscape must have been considerable, yet unless you know what you are looking for the embankment is difficult to spot today. Time heals many of the wounds which progress inflicts on the countryside, blending what may seem like permanent scars into the natural order. There is a happy legacy for the modern tourist which the railway builders could never have dreamed of, for even if the railway line was not built until the 1860s, and had far more to do with the development of mass tourism than with the more exclusive period with which this book is concerned, it now provides an ideal way of seeing the estuary on foot. The rails and sleepers have long since gone and the embankment along which the trains used to run is now owned by the

Snowdonia National Park who have turned it into the Morfa Mawddach Walk.

The distance from Barmouth to Dolgellau by this route is 9½ miles (15 km), but for those who prefer not to go the whole way it is possible to cross the bridge at Penmaenpool and reach the main road, where there is a bus service. To find the beginning of the walk you should leave Barmouth town centre by the Dolgellau road and take a footpath on your right which leads down onto the railway bridge. A small charge is made for crossing the footway, but once you begin to move out over the water the situation makes it worth every penny. At the southern end of the bridge, either turn left immediately along a ruined sea wall and then follow a rather complicated network of paths past Mawddach Crescent, or continue along the railway to Morfa Mawddach Station where you can pick up the disused track on the left of the platform. The latter alternative is easier to find, but far less interesting. For the rest of the way the walking is straightforward and easy, providing every opportunity to enjoy this uniquely beautiful stretch of countryside in perfect peace and quiet. The Snowdonia National Park has thoughtfully provided picnic places at intervals along the route.

Frances Kilvert arrived at Dolgellau by train the day before his ascent of Cadair Idris, and this brief note in his diary for the 12th. June 1871 catches the relaxed atmosphere of those early years of railway travel.

At 1 o'clock we started for North Wales. Just before we reached Barmouth Junction [Morfa Mawddach] the train was hailed and pulled up and a party of young people came tumbling into our carriage. It was Strong, Mary and Freddie and two Misses Davies. They were staying at Barmouth and had been out into the country to visit a friend who had influence enough to hail the train as if it were an omnibus and pull it up for them. From Barmouth Junction, leaving the sea we travelled up the beautiful valley to Dolgelley beside the noble estuary of the Mawddach, mountains standing close on either side of the river.

With the coming of the railways the age of mass tourism began, and a new generation of guidebooks developed to satisfy this rapidly growing market. The erudite style of the early tourists was replaced by a more down to earth approach, and with everything and everywhere now accessible, the emphasis was on completeness. Mr. Askew Roberts' *Gossiping Guide to Wales*, though it was published long after the days of the early tourists, is far too fascinating to be omitted from these pages. It has more in common with modern guidebooks than with the journals of men such as Bingley and Evans, which had been the main sources of information half a century before. Written specifically for railway travellers, it is designed to be read on the train, with descriptions of what can be seen out of the windows between stations, as well as suggested excursions from towns and villages served by the railway. Mr Roberts makes his purpose quite clear in the introduction to the 1884 edition.

My object by preparing this book has been to give Tourists a readable as well as practical Guide to the chief scenes of interest in North Wales —— something to talk about at every station they pass, when on the railways, and when they go off, a description of the objects they must by no means miss seeing.

Costing only a shilling [5p], with 208 pages and numerous illustrations, it packs in a great deal of information, together with lots of advertisements, which may well explain the modesty of the price. Looking at the typography, the simple but effective line illustrations, and above all the advertisements, recalls this period more surely than any written description ever could. The guide must have been printed in vast quantities and it is well worth keeping a look-out for copies which can occasionally be found in second-hand bookshops and jumble sales. It makes a fascinating companion, especially for those who already know the area well. When visiting the Panorama Walk recently I was able to identify the exact spot from which the illustrator had made his drawing of the Mawddach Estuary; a rather comfortable looking flat-topped boulder sheltered by an oak tree.

By the time that Mr. Roberts compiled his guide there was another change in the holiday-makers', attitude to their surroundings; the age of the fixed period, single destination holiday had begun. For the early tourists travelling on foot, on horseback, or by carriage, there was little chance of becoming bored. Travel was a challenging occupation in itself and had not yet become merely the routine means of reaching a destination, where you would remain for as long as you had booked accommodation. Writers like Bingley and Wyndham were concerned with travel for its own sake, and when they had seen as much as they wanted to in one place they moved on to another. The great success of Mr. Roberts's guide may have had something to do with his addressing the new problem of 'what to do on holiday', for he introduces a great deal of information which would have seemed quite extraneous to the writers who preceded him.

One exotic feature of this area during the nineteenth century was a minor gold rush, and many relics of this fickle industry remain. Mr. Askew Roberts's *Gossiping Guide* gives a contemporary account of one of them as seen from the Barmouth to Dolgellau railway line.

..... over the widening estuary we can see the chimney of the famous Vigra and Clogau Gold mine. Twenty years ago there was a regular gold fever in Merionethshire. The fever commenced about 1860, and in this way:— A Mr. Williams became the purchaser of the Vigra and Clogau Mine, which had been worked for copper for a considerable period [it was already a substantial mine in the 1790s]; but Mr. Williams tried for gold. Curious stories are told of the hopes, fears, and disappointments of the owner and his manager, John Parry, when, one morning - it is said on the very day they had agreed to abandon the search, ruin staring them in the face - Parry made such a discovery as turned the heads of the whole community. The excitement was pardonable, for, in a ' bunch,' he found what proved to be thirty-six thousand pounds' worth of gold! At once the fever raged. Nothing was thought of by day or dreamed of by night, but

> Gold! and gold! and gold without end,
> Gold to lay by, and gold to spend,
> Gold to give, and gold to lend,
> And reversions of gold *in futuro*.

Mines were opened in various places, and hopes ran high. But after a while the fever abated. The finding of the nuggets at Clogau was a piece of good fortune not to be repeated. True, that company did net a profit of £ 20,000 a year for two or three years after, and now and then makes a valuable haul of the precious metal still, but the other mines are abandoned.

The Clogau mine continued to operate until quite recently, but at the time of writing it has closed following the failure of a plan to develop it as a tourist attraction. It is still possible to see the workings at close quarters if you follow a footpath from Bontddu which is described in the appendix on longer walks at the back of this book as the termination of the walk from Tal-y-bont. A more sinister proposal in recent years was the plan put forward by a leading multinational company to dredge the whole of the estuary to recover gold and copper washed down from the surrounding hills. Fortunately this scheme was abandoned.

By 1790 Barmouth was already becoming a popular resort and the tourists' journals suggest that this was largely due to the efforts of one person. Most first time visitors were not favourably impressed by the town. They found that the sand carried from the beach by the prevailing westerly wind was a serious inconvenience, not only outside but also indoors, where it penetrated everything. The saving grace was Mrs Lewis at the original Corsygedol Inn, whose hospitable and well run establishment, together with the superb beach which made the town an ideal place to indulge in the relatively new fashion of sea bathing, had much to do with Barmouth's rapid development. This boost to the local economy was particularly important as the town's chief commercial asset, its harbour, was beginning to silt up.

The Reverend William Bingley's description of Barmouth, as quoted in Nicholson's *Cambrian Travellers Guide*, is perhaps unduly harsh, but even he soon became fond of the place.

Old Cottages, Barmouth

Barmouth, or Abermaw, in Merionethshire, is placed near the conflux of the river Maw, or Mawddach, in a situation wretchedly fitted for a town. The houses are disposed, either among the sand, in a low situation, or reared at different heights on the side of a huge rock, like part of the city of Edinburgh; and said to resemble the town of Gibraltar. These houses form 8 tiers, one range above another, to which there is no approach but by steps cut in the rock. The floor of one row is about level with the chimneys immediately in front, so that a person standing at his door, may look down the chimneys of the neighbourhood below. The first range regales the second with its smoke, the second the third, &c. till we arrive at the uppermost, which in a westerly wind, takes the mixed perfume of all.

Although the town is now consolidated at the base of the rock, its character is still very much as Bingley describes, and here and there the old houses remain; Pen-y-grisiau in the main street is a fine example. No visit to Barmouth can be complete without wandering up one of its steep lanes behind the main street until you can look down on the houses, and down their chimneys, with the whole of Cardigan Bay as a backdrop. A maze of alleys and paths connected by steps crisscross the hillside making it virtually inaccessible to motor vehicles, so that the atmosphere of the town which Bingley describes is preserved. It will come as a surprise to those who only know the centre of this busy resort that such a charming diversion is to be found within a few moments' walk.

In 1798 Bingley had been exploring the wilder regions of Wales for some weeks before he arrived here, and in spite of his initial reservations he eventually came to see it as an outpost of civilisation.

It is frequented during the summer season by many genteel families from Wales, and the west of England, as a sea bathing place . . .

The company must find it an uncomfortable place, for the inn (the Corsygedol Arms) is at times almost buried in the sands, and a person cannot walk many yards from the door without being up to the ankles in it. Added to this, a strong westerly wind blowing against the windows and into all the rooms, must render it horridly unpleasant. Where it not for the hospitable Mrs. Lewis, the place would fail in one of it's chief attractions.

I was beyond measure surprised upon being introduced into the dining room, to find upwards of thirty persons, most of them of fortune and fashion, in so secluded a corner of the kingdom. I found too, upon enquiry, that this was by no means all the company at that time in the town, for another large and good building, which Mrs. Lewis had in her own hands as a lodging house, was also quite full. To be again introduced, as it were into the world, after my solitary rambles amongst the wilds of this country, made a most pleasing variety in my tour; and I enjoyed very much the cheerfulness and affability of every one present. .....

Within the last three years, the number of visitors to this place has been much increased, which I can attribute to no other cause but the civility of the good hostess. She makes it her study to please everyone, and she is so fortunate as seldom to fail.

The novelty of communal eating appealed to many of the early tourists but not to John Byng, the future Lord Torrington. He made a brief visit 14 years earlier, when the influence of Mrs Lewis had not yet taken effect.

At our return, a room was found with two beds for our bodies; and a receptacle for our beasts. In a dirty parlour we placed ourselves; and were soon joined by other customers, the cloth was laid, and preparations made for supper, to which we sat down amidst a crew of blackguards, to whom it was difficult to know how to behave, or what to do.

My friend, who is all politeness, carv'd for, and drank to, these people; and, thus, we went on in our vulgarity, till a woman of the meanest dress and manners, forc'd herself on a chair by him; on which she tilted, with a coulour'd handkerchief spread before her; when I cou'd scarcely keep my countenance, nor dare look up to him.

Added to 4 or 5 vulgar fellows, of our society, there were three boys who ate for a wager. There was but one spoon, that served the several dishes. Eager to hasten from this party, I stole to our chamber & sent for Mr. P. to come up to me; when we (after some shy remarks) ventur'd into two miserable truckles, where sleep was forbidden; and I listen'd to the abuse of some men, who grudg'd us these charming beds: mine was shorter than anything I had yet enter'd.

Oh! how we did grunt and groan in the morning; as, have you slept? How I have sweated! I am weaker than a rat! Heigh ho! Let us be gone: and in half an hour we were gone, and with a guide, as the tide was coming in; and we had the sands to cross.

Had the fashionable set not yet discovered the place, or was John Byng just a snob? He toured extensively, both in Britain and on the Continent, and kept detailed records of his travels which were only published comparatively recently under the title of *The Torrington Diaries*. He was also a notable hypochondriac, and at that time travel was considered to be good for the health, though he does not seem to have sampled Barmouth's chief attraction, sea bathing, which was a recognised treatment for many illnesses. In those days swimming was not the informal matter that it has now become, and this may have as much to do with its association with medical treatment as with the moral climate of the time. At most fashionable resorts, entering the water was associated with special machines designed to provide privacy, and which required attendants to operate them. William Bingley, as a man of the cloth, only mentions the arrangements at Barmouth in passing:

There are at Barmouth, three bathing machines, but these are entirely appropriated to the use of the ladies, the gentlemen bathing on the open coast. The amusements seem to consist of going out in parties on the water, or in lounging on the sands or beach. The latter is one of the most delightful walks I ever beheld.

A year later Sir Robert Ker Porter took a rather more robust interest in the proceedings:

This is a gay place for bathing, here the ladies sans ceremonies stroll into the sea like Eve, with small raiment round their centres. Not a whole regiment of males with magnifying glass nor the surge of a Biseagan ocean could possibly, either call a blush to their bodies or wash this time embronzing innocence of custom. However this exhibition of mountains may be classed in natural beauty with Snowdon and Cader Idris.

If walking was an important part of the amusements at Barmouth in the early days of tourism, this activity was largely confined to the beach. The Panorama Walk, one of Barmouth's most famous attractions, was not created until later in the nineteenth century, and although it is now thought of as an excursion on foot from the town to a particular viewpoint overlooking the Mawddach estuary, the name originally referred to a series of terraces which were created on this hillside. Here fashionable visitors could wander sedately back and forth while admiring the view. They were as likely to reach this place by carriage as on foot, and they paid to enter the promenade where refreshments were available. Askew Roberts describes it in his *Gossiping Guide*.

Next in attraction are the magnificent mountain walks. The first nineteen out of every twenty tourists attempt is the one known as The Panorama Walk, and not a few miss the goal simply because they conceive that the highest ground must necessarily reveal the most extensive prospect. The shortest way up is by what we will call the Sylfaen Lane (For it leads to Sylfaen farm), which turns off the main road to the left, soon after passing the approach to the bridge; after walking up the lane for a quarter of an hour or so, a large gate crosses the road to be followed, while the road to be avoided forks to the left. In a short time we see the shoulders of two low hills before us, when we very speedily reach the guarded entrance to the "view," which is between a mile and a half and two miles from the hotels. The toll is a penny, and sometimes the public grumble, and "write to the papers," little knowing that but for the spirit and enterprise of Mr. Davids, of the Corsygedol Hotel, the view would have been lost to the public altogether. When we reach our goal all the glories of the Estuary are spread out before us, and we see the mountains we have already seen from the bridge, with others besides. Returning to the toll-wicket, we may there turn to the right and descend through the wood to the Dolgelly road, along which we walk back [1½m.] to the town.

Although the view from the original terrace is now partly obscured by trees, it is only necessary to go a little way beyond the end of it to see why this spot has become so famous. Our forbears may have needed a specially built promenade, with seats and refreshments, in order to appreciate fully the vast landscape spread out before them, but when it is seen from the open hillside, which provides an abundance of deep heather to lounge on, it loses nothing and is still one of the wonders of North Wales.

A slightly more arduous, but far more rewarding approach to the panorama than that suggested by Askew Roberts, can be made by starting in the centre of Barmouth and following the steep footpath which leads over the brow of the hill above the town, joining Sylvan Lane just before the right turn to the panorama which he mentions. When using this route you will not only have the opportunity to enjoy the views over the town but, a little further on, you will get a very good idea of the type of road which led to Barmouth before the new one was built along the shore at the end of the 1790s.

If the formal promenade had not yet been built when the Reverend John Evans reached Barmouth in 1798 there were other social delights awaiting him, and although some passages in his journal suggest a rather stuffy personality, he certainly did not suffer from John Byng's reservations about the informal atmosphere of the place.

The company, though not numerous, was genteel. Through the wetness of the season, few of the Shropshire and Herefordshire beauties had yet arrived; yet the place was expected soon to fill: this being the resort of the indolent and affected of the midland part of the kingdom, as Weymouth is for the western part.

Adjoining to the inn is a large boarding-house capable of containing a number of families. Here at one common table, which is well served, the company sit down to dinner and supper together, as at Matlock: an admirable harper is kept in pay. An assembly [dance] twice a week affords exercise and amusement for the evening; and the surrounding country furnishes objects for both during the day.

From the friendly footing on which strangers meet here, they resemble one great family, united for the purpose of social intercourse and mutual pleasure. The lodgings are good and the expenses moderate; and, when the price of provisions is taken into the account, it would be extortion were it not otherwise. Mutton three pence [1p] per pound; kid by the quarter the same; fowl ten pence [4p] to one shilling [5p] per couple; most kinds of fish ten pence [4p] to one shilling [5p] per pound.

Every consideration is heightened by the most pleasing attention from the hostess and her servants; so that he who cannot spend two or three months under the roof of Lowii Lewis, without experiencing ennui, must be possessed of a spirit not easily pleased: and has yet one of the most essential of human sciences to learn.

Sadly, many of the early tourists were oblivious to Welsh culture except when its 'foreign-ness' caused them inconvenience; however there was one exception to their indifference; this was music. In rural Wales, then as now, this means the harp and the human voice. By the beginning of the nineteenth century most of the larger inns and hotels had harpists who entertained the guests in the evenings, though the standard of performance was often uneven. As early as 1798 the Reverend Richard Warner, who was far more enthusiastic about Barmouth than Bingley (they visited the town at about the same time) was entranced by one particularly accomplished performer. His journal employs a common convention of the time, being written in the form of letters to a friend.

Before we quitted this enchanting spot yesterday morning, we had an opportunity of hearing the Welsh harp in perfection, the only time when we have met with an excellent player since we began our expedition .....

The name of the Barmouth harper is Parry, a young man who from the age of seven studied and practiced the instrument, and has attained to an uncommon excellence upon it.

You are aware, my dear sir, that the telyn, or Welsh harp, is very superior to the one common in England, having three sets of strings, the middle set comprising flats and sharps. * Mr. Parry's management of this powerful and flexible instrument is, indeed, very surprising; wether he wishes to sooth by softness, charm with delicacy, melt with pathos or rouse with energy, " the harp, obedient to the masters hand," produces irresistibly the desired effects. Struck by such a finger as this, you will imagine we heard with no small satisfaction, all the old Welsh popular airs, with variations adapted to them by the late celebrated Mr. Parry; but none pleased us so much as the one called Harlech Castle, wild, simple, and pathetic, beyond the power of language to describe.

* The ancient Welsh harp had only one row of strings, and these were formed of twisted hair. Towards the conclusion of the 15th.

century two other sets of strings were added, and gut was introduced in lieu of hair. Before this improvement the harper produced flats and sharps by a particular management of the finger and thumb, a much more difficult, as well as more imperfect method than now practiced.

Harpists still perform at some of the larger hotels during the summer season, and one is often to be found at Harlech Castle. For those modern tourists who do not wish to ignore Welsh cultural life, it is worth looking for posters advertising concerts by some of the local choirs. These performances are usually friendly and informal affairs, with a repertoire combining traditional folk songs and ballads with more cosmopolitan items.

Warner's favourable impression of Barmouth may well have been influenced by the spectacularly warm welcome he received from Mrs Lewis and her staff at the Corsygedol Hotel when he and his companions arrived late one evening, after walking from Harlech in a storm. He is careful to acknowledge his gratitude before ending the account of his stay, and such publicity as this, and in other books which became best sellers, must have done much to encourage future visitors.

It would be ungrateful in us not to acknowledge the extreme kindness of the landlady at our present quarters, the Corsygedol Arms, who, though her house is inconveniently full, received us (wet, dirty, and miserable as we appeared to be) with alacrity, and afforded us every possible comfort. The waiter and chamber-maid also must not be forgotten. The former has accommodated two of us with the contents of his wardrobe; and the latter furnished the rest of our party with petticoats, to supply the absence of the waiter's inexpressibles, which the disproportion in size between him and our other two friends prevented them from using.

The last sentence is ambiguous, and might lead the reader to speculate about Mr. Warner's fellow travellers. Although we know that he had three companions, unfortunately he neither names nor describes them.

The problem of hotels and inns being full became common soon after the beginning of tourism, and although more and more accommodation was created as the market increased, there never seemed to be quite enough to satisfy the periods of peak demand. This was partly because visitors were spending longer in one place, and by the time that Askew Roberts compiled his *Gossiping Guide* there had been an important change in the habits of visitors. Tourists were in the process of becoming holiday-makers.

Askew Roberts seems to have commissioned the long and detailed introductory sections of his book, which deal with general subjects such as history, geology, botany and conchology, entirely from clergymen. Perhaps their fees were more moderate than those of professional writers, but their enthusiasm for their subjects is overwhelming. In his chapter entitled 'A Botanical Ramble at Barmouth', the Right Reverend the Bishop of Bedford enters into the holiday spirit.

> There are few better places for a botanical ramble than Barmouth, and perhaps scarcely any in which so many scarce and interesting plants can be found within so small an area. We will suppose a party of ardent botanists to arrive (as the members of the Oswestry and Welshpool Naturalists' Field-club did once arrive) at the Barmouth station. Never mind the month. I am going to tell them what they may find, if they are lucky; but what they will find in blossom will no doubt depend on the time of year they select. Of course I cannot pretend to say what bits of waste ground with their treasures may be built over in the next few years, nor what rocks with their rarities may be blasted and carted off by builders. I can only talk of Barmouth as it is in this Year of Grace. 1876.

Do 'ardent botanists' from Oswestry still arrive at Barmouth station? If they do they will be aware that to pick and press wild

flowers within the town, if any are to be found, may land them in trouble, and they will probably confine themselves to note-taking and photography. On the other hand they will not need to wander further than the closest open hillside during the spring and summer months to find themselves surrounded by a vast range of species, and although the bishop's fear that new buildings would obliterate some of his favourite haunts was justified, he was quite wrong about the quarries. One of these can still be seen as you travel out of Barmouth on the Dolgellau road, and now being long disused, it is festooned with plants as well as supporting a raucous seagull colony. Even if the bishop's style is dated, his contribution still tells us much about the atmosphere of the town in years gone by, when nature and urban development were so intertwined that you could study one without leaving the environs of the other.

Returning to the early days of tourism, we may find that the impressions recorded in many of the journals are bland and romanticised; after all, if you are travelling for pleasure you are unlikely to dwell on the unpalatable realities of life. A rare exception occurs in the Reverend John Evans's account of his visit to a cottage outside Barmouth in 1798. This confronts the underbelly of a harsh society in which there was little provision for social services.

In one of my morning walks I took a little bye path, rendered less inviting by the stench of an adjoining pigs' cote. The weather was hot, and I had not yet dined. Had it not been for an obstinate and headstrong curiosity, that leads me to investigate and see if possible the end of every thing, and to study nature in her reclusest haunts, I should have made this an excuse for not proceeding farther. The cry of an infant at no great distance attracted my attention and hastened my steps. As I farther ascended the hill, a hut, little better than the cote I had left, forbade my approach. At the entrance, for door there was none, stood a tall female figure, which from her tattered dress and sallow countenance, you would scarcely have supposed to be human; with a distorted figure at her breast. I spoke, but she, not understanding my language, and little supposing that I would enter such a dwelling, still kept her post. I then took the child by the hand and pointed for admittance. The hut consisted of one room upon the ground floor; divided by a partition of lath and reeds. The floor was native soil, rendered very hard and uneven from long and uneven pressure. At the farther end was a fire of turf, laid upon a few stones; near which stood a three-legged stool, a small cast-iron pot, some branches of broom tied up for a besom, and a few bundles of rushes thrown down for a bed. These constituted the principal furniture! At the other end was a lank meagre figure sitting in a loom; the father of the family.

At this employment, after fourteen hours' toil, he could earn eight-pence [4p]. But a chronic illness, occasioned by low debilitating diet, prevented his following it so close as constantly to earn this. A similar cause prevented the wife from properly looking after four sickly children. The eldest was stunted in its growth; the second lame; the third blind; and the youngest, though two years old, still at the breast, and wasting away with the tabes dorsalis.

Entering farther into their history, I learnt that the linen trade had been much better and provisions cheaper; when they might, if Fortune had smiled, have done something; but owing to a very severe illness, in consequence of a bad lying in, the wife had been incapacitated for taking an active part in the business, as she used to do; and consequently they were unable to put any thing by for a day of adversity. The same cause precluded them the benefit of medical advice. Even when a transient appetite returned, they were destitute of the means to procure more than a coarse and scanty morsel, hardly sufficient to satisfy the immediate cravings of hunger. The world had no value in their estimation; their hearts grown callous to its concerns. In such a truly deplorable state, life itself appeared to have no charms; and death was looked on as a welcome messenger that would bring them consolation. They talked of it with cheerfulness, and seemed reanimated when I mentioned that state of retribution, where the sincere, though humble, Christian, "Shall have all tears wiped away; and sorrow and sighing should flee away."

You will readily suppose that I could not hear this distressing history without manifesting symptoms that my feelings were interested. My hand had involuntarily slid into my pocket; and I was about to offer a mite of charity before I had scarcely heard the tale to excite it. A thousand words you would have read in my countenance at that time; one moment I felt sympathy for the object around me — regret for not feeling more; and that I had not more ability to relieve their varied distress; then indignation at my species, to think that it could spend months and months in plenty, if not in luxury, without attempting to rescue their fellow creatures from such complicated misery.

Unable longer to witness distress which I could not effectually relieve, I blessed them with a feeble accent; promised that I would see them again , and on returning to the inn, found that I had beguiled the hour of dinner.

There is something chilling in the way he accepts the inevitability of this scene, and perhaps even a note of gloating sensationalism in his description of it. That, as he mentions in the last sentence, he had missed his dinner at the hotel, is an unintentional irony which amounts to callousness, but then Freud had not yet created the science which would allow his readers to evaluate the use of the word 'species' in the penultimate paragraph.

CHAPTER 4

THE MOUNTAINS AND THE SEA

The church at Llanaber

Modern tourists leaving Barmouth by car in the direction of Harlech will negotiate a steep, and in places narrow, road until they reach the outskirts of the town. Here, if the day is clear, they will be rewarded with a view over miles of sandy beaches backed by sand-dunes. The rolling hills of the Llŷn Peninsula can be seen in the distance, increasing in height and ruggedness as the eye sweeps from west to east, presenting visual crescendo which rises steadily towards the highest summits of Snowdonia. We have left the interior of Ardudwy with its deep valleys and grey crags, and have entered a world flooded with light, the vastness of the sea and the ever changing sky constantly drawing the eye.

During the next dozen or so miles the road seldom rises more than two hundred feet above sea level, winding through small villages and past developments which are the logical consequence of modern mass tourism. This is the heartland of Ardudwy, its economic core where the majority of the population is concentrated, and yet you only have to travel a mile inland at any point to reach some of the wildest and most unspoilt countryside in Wales. The coastal fringe is a place of violent contrasts, where ugliness is not hard to find, but where one is also closest to the origins of human settlement in the Ardudwy. If the sprawling caravan sites on the left-hand side of the road are intrusive, then one has only to look to the right to pick out some of the oldest and most beautiful farmhouses in the area. Rising above their jumbled barns and outbuildings, sheltered by stands of wind-distorted trees, they are easily identified among the neat modern houses which surround them. On the moors high above are hill-forts, standing stones and cromlechs, representing thousands of years of unrecorded history, but to see these it is necessary to do a little walking. These ancient sites were among the chief attractions for the early tourists. Thomas Pennant, Richard Fenton and others came here in the second half of the eighteenth century, not simply to marvel at them, but also as antiquaries intent on studying them systematically for the fast developing science of archeology.

Richard Fenton was a South Walian of Norman extraction who, after legal studies at Magdalen College Oxford, devoted most of his life to travel, always with the purpose of recording what he saw. In the early years of the nineteenth century he repeatedly left his estate in Pembrokeshire to make tours through North Wales, and the wealth of records which he left at his death are still valuable to researchers. By the standards of the day his notes were meticulous, and they tell us much about the ancient monuments with which we are familiar, but they also allow us to assess how much has disappeared in the intervening years. He was rare among the early tourists in that he spoke

Welsh, and he was often accompanied on his journeys by the aristocratic antiquary Sir Richard Colt Hoare, whose lifetime study of the twelfth century writings of Giraldus Cambrensis was complementary to Fenton's own interests. However he was not particularly impressed by what he saw when he travelled north from Barmouth one evening in 1800. Perhaps it was the weather.

> Leave Barmouth in the Evening, our road leading cut out [of] the side of a Hill over the Sands. Pass the church of Llanaber [Trans. the church by the river mouth] just on the edge of the steep over the Sands, and by its name, it implies that the mouth of the Estuary was nearer the Church formerly. It is an odd looking building. The bell hangs over the porch, the first I ever saw of that kind.

Had Fenton been familiar with the history of this magnificent building he would, no doubt, have been less dismissive. The site on which it stands is said to have been chosen by Saint Bodfan in the sixth century, and the original structure was probably of wood. The Celtic saints had a wonderful eye for landscape, and it is often worth visiting places with which they are associated for this reason alone. Llanaber is no exception, and from the terrace by the west wall one experiences a spectacular view over the bay. Extensive restoration in 1858 has made the church's antiquity less obvious from the outside, but once you have passed through the Gothic doorway you are left in no doubt as to the age of the building in which you stand. Massive Norman pillars flank the nave, and above them the lancet windows of the celestory direct the eye towards the chancel. This is probably the oldest part of the church, dating from around 1200 A.D. It has a connection with Cymer Abbey in that the present building was probably the work of Hywel ap Maredydd ap Cynan, Lord of Ardudwy, son of the same Maredydd ap Cynan whom the Cistercian monks considered to be one of their benefactors.

Maredydd is mentioned by Giraldus Cambrensis in the extract from his work which is quoted in Chapter 1.

But Fenton passed by with only a wry remark about the bell, and continued on his way to an Elizabethan mansion, a little farther along the coast, which for centuries had been the seat of one of the branches of the ubiquitous Vaughan family.

> An uninteresting Country all the way to Corsygedol, our place of destination for that night, there being an uniform tract of high sloping coarse ground, intersected with cold stone fences, and miserable patches of Corn here and there, and no trees but a few near some old house. This to the right of the road, and to the left a dead flat of moory meadows, degenerating first into Turbary [peatbog] to the Seas for S[outh] about a Quarter of a Mile; then the Ocean, with the Promontory of Llŷn. This flat extends all the way to the foot of the Hills to Llŷn, part of the same sort of Country as is said to have been inundated about the year 500, under the name of Cantref y Gwaelod.

The legend of Cantref y Gwaelod, or the Lowland Hundred, is one of the oldest and most romantic of the folk tales with which Ardudwy is associated, and there is no doubt that at the time of the early tourists it was still seen not as legend but as history. The Reverend John Evans, who passed this way sometime after Richard Fenton, gives the following version of the story.

> From the high ground above Corsygedol a good view is obtained at ebb tide of Sarn Badrwyg, or the ship-breaking causeway: so called from the dangers, which vessels are in, that approach this sunken reef of stones at full and half tide. It is an artificial work, running out south westerly far into the sea, about twenty-four feet thick. Sarn y Bwlch, which extends from a point north west of Harlech*, is supposed to have met the end of this, within which

* Fenton's geography is incorrect here, the Sarn y Bwlch lies some miles north-west of Aberdyfi.

boundary, or embankment, was comprised formerly a rich tract of land called Cantref Gwaelod or the low land hundred, well stocked and inhabited. The names of several towns are still preserved in the traditions of the Welsh, and the disaster is finely depicted in a beautiful elegiac poem, descriptive of the melancholy event.

About the year 500 it is said, at the time Gwydno Goranhir was lord of the territory, one of the wards of the sea-defence through intoxication, neglected the necessary precautions at the flood-gates in the dam, when the sea rushed through with such force as to blow up part of the wall, and overflow the whole hundred, which remains in the same inundated state to the present hour. An accident of this kind happened at some remote period on the coast of Essex. For it is a fact, that the usual prebend given to the canons of St. Paul's in London, to qualify them for becoming residentiaries, is, " the Prebenda consumpta per mare."

There is no question that Sarn Badrig exists, for at low spring tides parts of it are clearly visible, extending some seven miles out into the bay. However today it is generally accepted that this extraordinary reef, which is made up of large boulders, was formed by glacial action during the last ice age. But the folk memory of the lost villages lives on.

When I was a child, my grandmother told me that if I were to stand on the beach at Mochras, on a night of hard frost when the moon was full, I might hear the bells of the drowned churches still ringing under the sea. I certainly wanted to believe her, but I was never able to visit Mochras when the conditions were right. With the passing years came scepticism, and it was only recently, when I looked at a chart of the coast, that I realised how much of what she had told me was true. The most powerful tides coincide with the new and full moons, and frosty weather is windless, allowing sound to travel for immense distances, especially if you are standing at the water's edge. The ebb and flow of these spring tides causes massive turbulence around the tip of the Llŷn Peninsula, and the races and overfalls this creates have long been feared by mariners. One race, which extends for many miles south east from Bardsey Island, is called the Devil's Tail and at spring tides its action is violent enough to set up a constant swell over much of the northern part of Cardigan Bay. Seven miles out from the shore at Mochras is a buoy marking the end of Sarn Badrig, and in the days before lights were installed on buoys, this would have had a bell on it which was kept in constant motion by the waves, to warn sailors of its presence at night. Had I visited Mochras on a perfectly still night with a full moon, then I would surely have heard a bell tolling for those lost villages, inundated one stormy night so long ago.

The name which Evans uses for this reef, Sarn Badrwyg, is not the one which you will find on modern maps. Now, probably as a result of non-Welsh speaking cartographers, it is known as Sarn Badrig or St. Patrick's Causeway, and many people will tell you that it is the Welsh end of the Irish causeway of the same name, which that intrepid evangelist crossed when spreading Christianity during the dark ages. The earlier version would seem more apposite as '*bad*' can mean 'boat' in Welsh and '*rhwyg*' means 'rend, tear, rupture or split'.

Richard Fenton's notes illustrate the precise nature of the danger which this reef posed to ships.

It seems that this Sarn is composed of detached Masses of Stones, now rounded as if rolled together from time to time by the agitation of the water, but as if it was the relic of some Work of Art, supposed to be done when that flat of Cantref Gwaelod was in being. Mr Owen told me he saw a West India Vessel strike on it and wrecked, but the Crew was saved.

They were lucky, for this was only one of countless vessels which were destroyed on Sarn Badrig in the days of sail, with great loss of life.

The main attraction in this area for Richard Fenton was undoubtedly the archaeological remains in the hills behind Corsygedol, and his attention had almost certainly been drawn to these by Thomas Pennant's description of them. Though Fenton's notes make it clear that he does not always agree with his predecessor's conclusions, he must have realised that Pennant, more than anyone else, was responsible for attracting the scientific world's attention to the wealth of antiquities awaiting study. The morning after his arrival at Corsygedol he set off to visit them for the first time, and their fascination would cause him to return to this area again and again.

> Monday, . . . 1800, attended by Mr. Owen the Rector of Llanenddwin, to which Llanddwa [Llanddwywe] is the chapel of ease, we rode above Corsygedol House into a large Field, covered with marks of old enclosures in all directions, and of all shapes and sizes, interspersed with Heaps of Stones in a circular form, like Carneddau, among which there was one surmounted by a large flat incumbent Stone resting on one place edgewise, evidently making one side of a Cistvaen, there existing another side, two gone. These works appear to have stretched over a vast tract of Ground, and might have extended to the eastward of the first Field we traversed, wherein the great works had been, quite to ye Base of a small Mountain called to this day Craig y Dinas, the Rock of the City; for there can be scarce doubt of there having been an old British Town, and that all the irregular works we saw are traces of early population, and that the circular heaps are chiefly sepulchral. I think this the place of which Pennant says there are such remains of Druidical Establishment, such as circles, Cromlechs, &c., totally mis-representing and mistaking the matter.

The Reverend John Evans published his massive tome, *The Beauties of England and Wales* in 1812, and the Welsh part of this fascinating compendium is an expanded version of his first book, *Letters written During a Tour Through Wales in the Year 1798*. His comprehensive description of the archaeological sites in this area mentions two circles which have virtually disappeared since his visit. He approached them from the north-east, after visiting Llyn Hywel and Llyn Bodlyn.

A cromlech Dyffryn Ardudwy

On the open plain in which these, and another small lake, called Llyn Irddyn are numerous druidical remains, forming a very rare group of this class of antiquities. First appear two circles, formed of loose stones; one about fifty-six feet in diameter and the other of smaller dimensions, both have large upright stones placed at intervals among the lesser ones. Half a mile from these are two carnedds of prodigious size, on the side of a hill. At the east end is a large cromlech composed of two incumbent stones, one placed over the edge of the other, resting upon five uprights, in an inclining position: the highest end of which measures seven feet from the ground, and the lowest near five. Near this is another carnedd or heap of stones; and in, or rather upon it, is a large cromlech supported by upright stones; a little further on [from] the same heap is another most magnificent cromlech, the tabular stone being twelve feet long, by nine broad. Four maeni hirion, or upright columns, from the height of ten feet, to twelve feet eight, accompany these cromlechs; three have fallen and one has retained its erect position. Several of those supposed religious vessels called cistian vaen; or stone chests, are seen lying around. Perhaps in no part of Britain is there still remaining such an assemblage of relics belonging to the druidical rites and customs as are found in this place, and the adjacent parts.

The cromlechs which Evans refers to are called Carneddau Hengwm and can be visited by leaving the A496 on either of the two footpaths which lead eastwards about a mile south of Tal-y-bont. If you use both paths you can make a circuit which affords superb views of the sea and the mountains. Indeed this excursion is worthwhile even if you are not interested in archaeology, but for those who are, a fuller account of the origins of human activity in Ardudwy is provided by an appendix at the back of this book. The carneddau are not particularly easy to find, and a suitable map of the kind recommended in the section on walks is essential. Both paths are steep in places, and you must expect to cross some boggy ground. If you complete the whole circuit you will pass Pen y Dinas (also known as Dinas Gortin), a large hill fort occupying a dramatic position on an exposed hilltop above Hendre Eirian. You will also find a homestead and stone circle about a quarter of a mile above Carneddau Hengwm. An even finer stone circle is to be found on the hillside above Egryn Abbey. Sadly the two large stone circles which Evans visited on his way to Carneddau Hengwm have all but disappeared, probably victims of wall building in the days before any protection was given to ancient monuments. They are clearly marked on the Ordnance Survey map, and their outline can still be detected on the ground, allowing the imagination to reconstruct them in all their majesty. If you wish to extend your walk to include this site, then you should follow the path above the carneddau until it joins the track from Bwlch y Rhiwgyr, from which point you can return via Pont Fadog to Tal-y-bont.

This is an area of small fields separated by stone walls, and careful attention should be paid to the map. If you find that further progress is barred by a dry-stone wall, with no stile or gate, then you have lost your way and should backtrack until you find it again. Hill farmers have little patience with trespassers whom they catch climbing walls, and rightly so. Although these structures look substantial, and will stand for generations if left undisturbed, they are no more than well organised piles of stones, held together by gravity and the skill with which they are built. Just one person climbing over can disturb the precise lay of the stones in a way which will lead to collapse, and hours of back-breaking and expensive labour for the owner.

Craig y Dinas is easier to find, and presents a less demanding walk. Leave the A496 coast road on the old Corsygedol drive (marked Fordd Cors on the O.S. map), and park near a gate just past some farm buildings. A brief diversion along the tarmacked road on your right will bring you to Coetan Arthur, a vast slab supported on a single column. Legend has it that this was thrown down from the summit of Moelfre by King Arthur; hence the name Arthur's Coit. Returning to the hill track which leads towards Llyn Bodlyn, follow it for about a mile and a half when you can turn right along the summit of the ridge which leads to Craig y Dinas. By keeping to the very crest of this ridge you will find the rather inconspicuous stone stile in the wall which surrounds the hill top. This commanding site provides a panoramic view through 360 degrees, and the wonderfully preserved walls of the fort ensure that there is always a place where you can shelter from the wind and enjoy it. With binoculars it is possible to pick out many of the sites mentioned by the early tourists, but at the time of their building the landscape would have looked very different. Pollen analysis tells us that they would have occupied clearings in dense hazel and alder woods, which were later cleared for agriculture and reduced to moorland by grazing. Our generation is not the first to alter vast areas of the landscape.

If, when you rejoin the track after visiting the fort, you continue a little further towards Llyn Bodlyn, you will find a boggy path on your right which leads down to the enchanting pack horse bridge of Pont Sgethin. From here it is possible to return to Corsygedol by way of Pont Fadog, which spans the River Sgethin in the sheltered oak woods above Tal-y-bont. This is a wonderful example of eighteenth century craftsmanship in stone which time seems to have forgotten; the builder's initials are inscribed on the parapet. It is well worth the detour to experience what travel on roads in Ardudwy was like two hundred years ago. You can also visit Craig y Dinas while following the walk from Tal-y-bont to Bontddu which is described in the appendix dealing with longer excursions.

With the exception of Coetan Arthur, it is necessary to walk over rough ground to visit any of the sites already mentioned. Fortunately, for those who prefer not to do this, there are two very fine cromlechs within 100 yards of the main road. These are to be found behind the primary school at Dyffryn Ardudwy, and they are clearly signposted.

If Richard Fenton's theory about a vast prehistoric town on the moors was somewhat fanciful, then the Reverend William Bingley was more sceptical when he visited the area in 1798.

A few hundred yards beyond the fifth mile stone, and at a little distance on the left of the road, were two cromlechs very near each other, placed on barrows, or heaps of loose stones, the supposed interments of some men of ancient note, the largest twelve feet long, and the quoit or upper stone, about twenty inches thick. I was told that this part of Merionethshire abounded in different species of Druidical antiquity.

Though these barrows, on account of the cromlechs erected on them, have every appearance of high antiquity, yet I am inclined to suppose, with Mr. Wyndham, a judicious traveller through this country in 1774, that many of the heaps of stones, usually taken for barrows or cairns, " were originally piled together for no other reason than that the rest of the field might provide the clearer pasture." ..... The mode of forming these ancient barrows or Carneddau, as they are called by the Welsh, was somewhat curious. When the carnedd was considered as the honourable tomb of a warrior, every passer by threw an additional stone out of reverence to his memory; but when this heap came to be disgraced by being the mark where the guilty was laid, the custom of every one who passed by, to fling his stone was continued; but now only as a token of detestation.

Continuing northwards we soon arrive at the small village of Llanbedr, with its beautiful old bridge over the Artro. Surprisingly, at the time of the early tourists this place seems to have attracted little attention, but by 1847 John Hicklin, in his *Illustrated Hand-book of North Wales*, has no hesitation in recommending it.

The next place reached is the village of Llanbedr with the river Artro running through it. Here is a good roadside inn, called the Victoria, where good accommodation will be met with. It is a very central spot for fishermen to locate, and also for the antiquarian. The Druidical and Celtic remains, Cromlechs, &c., are most numerous, and there are various rivers and lakes up in the mountains. The narrow verdant dell of Cwm Bychan and lake, which is encompassed with precipitous rocks and black and dreary scenery, can be easily visited from here, and the route may be continued over the mountains to Harlech, affording a great variety of mountain scenery.

This charming village marks an important crossroads for tourists, giving access to Cwm Nantcol and Cwm Bychan to the east, and the tidal island of Mochras to the west. Whereas the coast road is, for the most part, a fast modern highway, if you turn inland at any point you will quickly find that in motoring terms the clock has been put back by many years. Single track roads are the norm, and with this narrowing of the carriageway comes a change of pace and atmosphere.

For a description of the valleys behind Llanbedr I have turned to Thomas Pennant, who was a Welsh speaking Welshman. This is partly because his is the most complete description of this very important area, but also because nearly all the early tourists who followed him use parts of his account. The publication of his two volume *Tours in Wales* did much to draw the attention of the touring classes to this as yet largely unvisited part of their own island. The 'Advertisement of the Author', which prefaces the first volume, published in 1778, explains Pennant's objectives and provides a glimpse of his working methods.

These home-travels are the first part of an account of my country.

They make of themselves a complete tour of the tamer parts of our country. In a future volume, the wild and romantic scenery will be presented, intermixed with the rich valleys so frequently interspersed. To which will be added an Appendix, containing the subjects referred to in this volume, with variety of other matter. I implore the aid of my countrymen to assist me in the attempt; and to favour me with the necessary materials. They will see that the great part of Denbighshire, and all parts of the four remaining counties of our principality, are still to be described. My frequent journeys through them, render me a tolerable master of their topography. I look up to my friends for history and anecdote latent among their papers; or references to our writers, lest any facts lodged in books might escape my memory.

Pennant can hardly be described as a tourist in the strict sense of the word, even if he did publish the record of his travels under the title *Tours in Wales*. He was a scientist with an international reputation, and although there is little doubt that he derived much pleasure from his researches in Wales, his primary objective was to make a meticulous record of the historical, social, cultural and topographical heritage of his homeland. This vast work was based on extensive travels throughout North Wales from 1773 to 1776, describing a way of life which would soon begin to change rapidly. Two centuries later it is still of great value, for although the speed with which he set down his thoughts led to the occasional slip, the results of

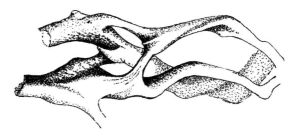

his research are presented in a clear and unpretentious style, which is extremely readable. Indeed his spontaneity makes his work particularly valuable to scholars as a faithful record of Wales at this time.

From Corsygedol, I pursued my journey towards Harlech; but, on the road, was tempted, by my constant fellow-traveller, the reverend John Lloyd, to make a small deviation to visit a near relation of his, who lived a few miles to our right, in his ancient territories of Cwm Bychan. We approached it from Glyn Artro, a little valley, watered by the river of the same name, and prettily wooded. The view upwards was extremely picturesque, of a conic rock, skirted by a sweet grove; and beyond soared the naked mountains, which bounded the object of our ride.

After passing through the wood, and ascending Dinas Pochellyn, we had before us a wild horizon of rocks and rocky mountains.

Even these tracts, unfriendly as they seem to vegetation, had once been covered with venerable oaks; and there still remain a few, between eight and nine feet in circumference. We went under the shade, above a rapid torrent with a delightful view before us of a true wooden Alpine bridge, and a small mill; and, a little farther, an ancient arch, flung from rock to rock, giving passage over a still and black water, shaded by trees. Ford the river again near Llyn Sarph, or The Serpent's Hole. Wind up a rocky staircase road, and arrive full in sight of Cwm Bychan, embosomed with rocks of magnificent height. After a short ride, high above a lake of the same name, descend, and reach the house of the venerable Evan Llwyd, who, with his ancestors, boast of being lords of these rocks, at least since the year 1100.

For the most part the valley is still as beautiful and unspoilt as it was in Pennant's day, although it is now possible to drive all the way to the end of the lake. Here you will find one of the most attractive parking places in the area, in a green meadow in front of Evan Llwyd's farmhouse. The 'ancient arch', which Pennant mentions, is probably the bridge at Cwm yr Afon, and for those who prefer to walk to the head of the valley, this is a good place to leave the car and complete the journey on foot. There is a choice of either following the road, or taking a more arduous route by crossing the bridge and then climbing steeply up old mine tracks to the lake of Gloyw Lyn at 1300 ft (400 metres). There follows an even steeper descent on a rough path to the bottom of the famous Roman Steps, from which point Cwm Bychan is approached from the south-west. Either route forms a fitting prelude to the dramatic scenery which Mr Bingley described in 1798. He is typical of the authors who where influenced by the 'cult of the picturesque', and his description makes a sharp contrast with Pennant's more factual but equally evocative account.

Cwm Bychan is a grassy dell, about half a mile in length, surrounded with the most black and dreary scenery imaginable. On the right of the entrance into it, is a small pool, called Llyn y Cwm Bychan, from whose edge Carreg y Saeth, the rock of the arrow,* towers, the blackest of the vale. I rested myself for a while on a rock, above the pool from whence I could at ease observe, and enjoy the rugged beauties of this romantic hollow. From hence the landscape extended in all it's magnificence: the vale was seen embosomed in stupendous rocks, black and barren, and enlivened only by the patches of meagre vegetation, lodged on their shelving precipices.

We descended into the hollow, and wandered along the bottom, till we came to the mansion (a true specimen of an ancient seat of a Welsh gentleman) lately occupied by Mr. Evan Lloyd, a person mentioned with much respect by Mr. Pennant's tour.

* Probably the ancient sportsmen took here their station to watch the passing deer, which formerly abounded in these parts.

This passage illustrates the change in the perception of landscape which has taken place over the last two hundred years. Surprisingly, Bingley's description of the scenery at Cwm Bychan as being 'black and dreary' would have been taken as a recommendation to visit the place by his contemporaries. They would have considered it to be sublime, awe inspiring, with a feeling of threat or impending doom which was an attractive ingredient in a 'picturesque scene', adding piquancy to the emotions which it inspired. But underlying this titillation was a very real dread of remote and barren countryside. This was an age when the Bible played a far greater part in education than it does today, and throughout the Scriptures the words 'desert' and 'wilderness' are used as powerful metaphors for suffering and divine retribution. There is no doubt that the early tourists' apprehension in such places was one of the aspects of the Welsh landscape which they found attractive. They could enjoy a slight frisson of fear when they experienced wild mountain scenery whereas their predecessors had only been intimidated and depressed by it. Because they were living at the dawn of an age in which man would begin to master and then dominate his environment, they could experience wild landscapes with a growing sense of security. This process has continued and developed up to the present day, and to a point which men such as Bingley could never have dreamed of. To a great extent man can now control his environment, and the consequences are one of the chief causes of concern among ecologists today.

Pennant's visit pre-dates such aesthetic posturings and it is a relief to return to the lucid account of the place which his scientific mind provides. As a Welshman, accompanied by a relative of the owner of Cwm Bychan, he was able to put the splendour of this beautiful place into an historical and social context in a way that Bingley could not have done. Their reception at the Llwyd's farmhouse was evidently a warm one, and Pennant soon broached two subjects with his host which were particularly engrossing for an eighteenth century antiquary: ancient history and genealogy.

This, and the fortified pass of Drws Ardudwy, were most probably occupied by the sons of Cadwgan, in their contests with the sons of Uchtryd ap Edwyn, whom they at last expelled the country.

The following, as it is the true descent of Mr. Evan Llwyd, and my fellow-traveller, who being brothers children, are eighteenth in descent from Bleddyn ap Cynfyn, so it is the genuine copy of the form of a British pedigree:

Evan ap Edward, ap Richard, ap Edward, ap Humphrey, ap Edward, ap Dafydd, ap Robert, ap Howel, ap Dafydd, ap Meirig Llwyd o Nannau, ap Meirig Vychan, ap Ynyr Vychan, ap Ynyr, ap Meuric, ap Madog, ap Cadwgan, ap Bleddyn, ap Cynfyn, prince of North Wales and Powys.

I was introduced to the worthy representative of this long line, who gave me most hospitable reception, in the style of an ancient Briton. He welcomed us with ale and potent beer, to wash down the Goch yr Weden, or hung goat, and the cheese, compounded of the milk of the cow and sheep. He likewise showed us the family cup, made of a bull's scrotum, in which large libations had been made in days of yore. The family lay in the whole store of winter provisions, being inaccessible a great part of the season, by reason of snow. Here they have lived for many generations without bettering or lessening their income; without noisy fame, but without any of its embittering attendants.

Of this house was the valiant Dai Llwyd, to whom is said to have been addressed the noted Welsh tune Ffarwel Dai Llwyd, on occasion of his going with Jasper Tudor and Owen Lawgoch, to fight Risiart Frawdwr, or Richard the traitor, by which name the Welsh stigmatised Richard the Third.

The mansion is a true specimen of an ancient seat of a gentleman of Wales*. The furniture rude: the most remarkable are the Cistiau Styffylog, or the oatmeal chests, which held the essential part of the provision.

The old farmhouse at the end of the lake still has a mellow permanence about it, and the minor changes which have taken place over the years have done nothing to impair its rudimentary charm. Modern visitors would be surprised if their host offered them hung goat, but they might also be deprived of a gastronomic treat. An extract from C. F. Cliffe's *Book of North Wales*, first published in 1821, describes a visit to Cwm Bychan, and brings this reference to life in a rather alarming way.

We witnessed not long ago, in the month of August, an event worth narrating, in this solitude. Whilst ascending we heard much shouting, and barking of dogs, intermingled with piercing shrieks. Then we passed a gigantic snow-white billy-goat, with his legs tied, struggling at intervals convulsively, and uttering very shrill cries.

*Note Bingley's use of the same phrase.

Presently we came in sight of Mr. Lloyd and several of his men, in a narrow part of the Pass, striving to capture another white billy-goat, of greater size, and even longer horns. The animal had taken refuge, after a long chase, on a very narrow ledge in the precipice, and apparently bid defiance to his pursuers, who for more than an hour tried with a sort of lasso, and sometimes by climbing at great risks as far as was practicable, to catch or dislodge him. The cunning with which the venerable looking goat ducked his head, as the looped rope struck his horns, was very entertaining; and the shouts of the men, the danger incurred by some, the excitement and barking of half a score of dogs, rivetted ones attention. At last, during a lull, billy thought he saw a chance of escape, and jumped down to a lower ledge; a renewed assault was made, during one of the pauses of which he bounded suddenly from a great height, and ran rapidly over bracken rocks and heath for about 600yds., with the pack of dogs close at his heals, who ultimately brought him up, but were kept at bay by the horns. (Goats can run nearly as fast as a dog). Two or three men, who were posted near the line of flight, now crept stealthily on, and lowering ropes round the poor creature's horns, secured him safely. Billy-goats are usually killed when three years old, at which age they are in good condition, and in August the flesh is not rank. The salted flesh, or hung goat, Coch yr Wden, is not used by those who wish to eat it in perfection, until three years afterwards. A number of goats are kept on these hills; and goats and sheep are sometimes killed by falling over the terrible steeps we have indicated.— Two large kites soared above the head of the pass.

Feral goats are still a common sight on the hills surrounding the lake, and there is some concern that, now that they are no longer used for food, there is an over-population problem. If, as would seem likely, hung goat was prepared in the same way as Jambon de Montagne in France or Prosciutto in Italy, it is possible that Welsh cuisine has lost a very great delicacy. Even if one recoils at the very thought of killing and eating such animals, there can be no doubt that life at the head of this remote valley would have been an austere business two hundred years ago, and that no source of food could possibly have been ignored. However Pennant's description makes it all sound idyllic.

The territories dependent on the mansion, extend about four miles each way, and consist of a small tract of meadow, a pretty lake swarming with trout, a little wood, and very much rock; the whole forming a most august scenery. The meadows are divided by a small stream, and are bounded on one side by the lake; on the other, by his woods, which skirt the foot of the rocks, and through which the river runs, and beyond them tumbles from the heights, in a series of cataracts. He keeps his whole territory in his own hands; but distributes his hinds among the Hafodtys, or summer-dairy houses, for the conveniency of attending his herds and flocks: he has fixed his heir on another part of the estate. His ambition at one time led him to attempt draining the lake, in order to extend his landed property: but, alas! he gained only a few acres of rushes and reads; so wisely bounded his desires, and saved a beautiful piece of water. He found on one side a stratum of fine white earth, about half a yard thick, which I perceived was what mineralogists dignify with the name of Lac Lunae, and Agaricus Mineralis*. The Germans use it as an absorbent in dysenteries and malignant fevers; and it would prove a good manure.

Stools and roots of firs, of vast size, are frequently found near the lake. Mr. Llwyd observed one, with the marks of fire on it, which he used to repair the Tyddyn y Traian, or jointure-house of his family; an ancient customary appendage to most of the Welsh houses of any note.

Among the Mountains which guard the Cwm, is one named Carreg y Saeth, on whose verge is a great Maen Hir, and Carnedd. Saeth signifies an arrow; so probably the ancient sportsmen here took their stand, to watch the passing of the deer, which formerly abounded in these parts. Nor have they long been extinct; a person

* A friable variety of chalk.

of the last generation informed my host, that he had seen eighteen at once, grazing in the meadow.

Though there are still trout in Cwm Bychan they are now scarce and small, a problem which effects many hill lakes in this area. The cause of this is thought to be a general rise in the acidity of the water since the industrial revolution, and several angling organisations have experimented with releasing chalk into their fisheries in order to counteract this effect. It is possible that the seam of 'white earth' mentioned by Pennant had something to do with Cwm Bychan being packed with trout in his day, and that when Mr Llwyd lowered the level of the water this no longer found its way into the lake, accelerating the increase in acidity.

With one exception, this valley has been spared the intrusion of twentieth century development. This is a wall which has been built round a most beautiful waterfall just below the lake, a glimpse of which used to be a very special pleasure when approaching Cwm Bychan. Its purpose seems to be solely to prevent people picnicking, as they have done for generations, beside the road at this idyllic spot.

When he left the Lloyd's farm, Pennant returned to Harlech without experiencing one of the great attractions at Cwm Bychan for modern tourists; the Roman Steps. For an eighteenth century traveller this fine example of the dreaded 'staircase path' would hardly have been a novelty. Before the building of turnpikes at the end of the eighteenth century these were a common means of communication, and it is places such as this which gave Welsh roads such a wicked reputation. The path which winds its way up Bwlch Tyddiad, on the shoulder of Rhinog Fawr, is now thought to be medieval in origin, not Roman, and is one of the few remaining examples which have not been overlaid by tarmacked roads. Walking on them is not

The Roman Steps, Cwm Bychan

unpleasant; riding a sure footed horse on them must have been slow and nerve racking; but to have travelled over such a pass in a carriage must have been a premonition of hell. Though there is no record of any of the early tourists trying to cross this particular staircase path by carriage they certainly faced similar obstacles between Tan-y-bwlch and Aberglaslyn, and wrote with feeling in their journals about the experience. Now the Roman Steps is one of the most poplar mountain walks in the area, and justly so. The Reverend William Bingley gives the essence of its appeal in his description, although once again he rather overdoes the gloom.

Having passed the mansion, we ascended on the other side, till we came to a deep mountain hollow, called Bwlch Tyddyad. Here the rocks close, and oppose a collection of shattered precipices, forming a scene of defoliation and barren-ness throughout. A few grasses, liverwort, and heath, constitute all the vegetation of this place. We wandered on this rocky cleft, for such it only seemed, till we got beyond the high mountains, when on a sudden, a fine open prospect of all the country eastwards was extended before us. Here we were treated with a pastoral landscape, bounded by high and distant mountains, which formed a majestic barrier around: amongst these, Cadair Idris, and the two Arrennigs were particularly conspicuous.

From hence we made a sharp turn to the right, still continuing our journey over a wretched horse path, ...

In recent years, extensive repairs have been made to the lower section of the path, so it is only in the upper section, beyond a wall with a gate in it, that you experience the original surface. The summit of the pass (allow 1hr from the car park) makes the long ascent worthwhile, though it is necessary to go a little way down the farther side to see the best of the view. Those who wish to climb Rhinog Fawr can take a path to the right, beside a wall some way short of the highest point. This will lead them up steep ground, past Llyn Du, to the summit in about an hour, and is not quite as intimidating as G. J. Bennett's 1837 account in *The Pedestrian Guide Through North Wales* suggests. He was an actor by profession, and may well have decided to cash in on the potentially profitable vogue for 'tours' while he was 'resting'. When his party of elegant young ladies and gentlemen from Corsygedol reached the top of the pass:

......suddenly we halted on hearing the distant halloos of travellers ascending the opposite side of the mountain; and presently three persons, one of whom was leading a wearied animal by the bridle, became distinctly visible.......

By their advice, we ascended the summit of the mountain, the view from which was grand and extensive. To the eastward, a vast country lies beneath, bounded by Cader Idris, the two Arrenigs, and a long range of mountains. Immediately under the lofty eminence, upon which we rested, was a small round lake, and the pass Ardydwy, which exceeds even the celebrated Llaberris in rugged grandeur. The way by which our new companions ascended was both laborious and dangerous; but they would not have sacrificed the prospect now presented to them on any account. North and south the eye glances over the summits of wild mountains, and to the west the Carnaevonshire chain, cut in two, as it were, by a high mountain, immediately before us, forms the shore of a noble piece of water, resembling a spacious lake, where the sea stretches its arm, into the vale of Maentwrog, out of Cardigan Bay. The declining sun gave us warning that it was time to quit these wilds, and make the best of our way to the foot of the mountain.

The return is extremely hazardous on horse-back. The ladies of the party, therefore, resigning their steeds to the conduct of some mountaineers, and the gentlemen leading their horses by the bridle, commenced the descent. But as I could not, from lameness, advantage myself by like caution, and feeling confident in the tact, strength, and docility of my favourite [horse], I led the way, without experiencing the least symptom of unease.

The classic traverse of the Roman Steps does not include the ascent of Rhinog Fawr, but involves a short, steep descent into a forestry plantation on the eastern side of the pass, before turning west through the Drws Ardudwy. This route, and the ascent of Rhinog Fawr, are described in full in the appendix dealing with longer walks. Mr Bingley passed this way and the latter part of his journey made a deep impression on him.

...... soon afterwards, turning again to the right, we entered another deep glen, called Drws Ardudwy, 'the pass of the overflowed land', a place well calculated to inspire the timid mind with horror. The sides and bottom were almost covered over with loose fragments of stone, once detached by the force of frost, after storms and heavy rain, from the heights above. The fear for personal safety must sometimes, in places similar to this, be accompanied with a tremor, for the mind is not always able to divest itself of prejudices and disagreeable associations of ideas, and in spite of every effort of reason and judgement, the unpleasing sensations of terror will sometimes affect us.

Even that hardy traveller Thomas Pennant was intimidated by this place, though one cannot help wondering if his fears were inspired by a genuine concern for his safety, whereas Bingley's had more to do with the cult of the picturesque.

This country is in the hundred of Ardudwy. The entrance to it from Trawsfynnydd is called Drws Ardudwy, formed by nature through the sterile mountains, which separate the districts. I was tempted to visit this noted pass, and found that the horror of it far exceeded the most gloomy idea which could be conceived of it. The sides seemed to have been rent by some mighty convulsion into a thousand precipices, forming at their tops rows of shelves, which the peasants, comparing to the ranges in a dove-cot, style Carreg y Clommenod, or the rock of the pigeons. The bottom of this passage is covered with a deluge of stones, which have streamed from the sides; and along it is a narrow horse-path, on the slippery rock, formed by a few of the fragments, which, in other places, are disposed into the shape of most steep and hazardous flights of steps: and yet, as if the natural and artificial difficulties of these ways were not sufficient to terrify invaders, there are, in one place, the vestiges of a wall, which went across the pass, in which might have been the door which gave name to it.

Though undoubtedly a dismal place to find oneself in bad weather, the Drws Ardudwy is not dangerous, but it is a remarkable feature which well deserves a visit. It can, of course, be approached relatively easily from the Cwm Nantcol end by those who do not want a long walk. If you are doing this you will start near an ancient farm called Maesygarnedd, which always seems to have a slightly sinister atmosphere, partly because of the remoteness of its situation, but mainly because of its association with a man who had a king's blood on his hands. As Pennant says;

> On my return, I visited an ordinary house, called Maesygarnedd, the birth-place of the regicide Colonel Jones; whose insolence to the neighbouring gentry is still spoken of, even to this day, with much warmth. Actuated by enthusiasm, he went every length that the congenial Cromwell dictated; and was a brave and successful officer in a cause, which, after a certain period, was the result of ambition, and the foundation of tyranny.

Not only was he a signatory to Charles I's death warrant, but he was Cromwell's brother-in-law, and an administrator who exerted considerable political influence in his day. According to *Lewis's Topographical Dictionary of Wales*, published in 1833, he was buried in Llanenddwyn churchyard at Dyffryn Ardudwy after being executed in 1660. There would seem to be some doubt over Pennant's sweeping condemnation of him, for although he was considered to be a traitor to the cause of Welsh independence, he also had a reputation for being on the side of small farmers and against speculators in matters of land reform, and was certainly a generous and understanding landlord in times of famine. At the time when Pennant visited Maesygarnedd, Colonel Jones's reputation probably depended on who was telling you the tale; after all it was little more than a hundred years since his death.

Although Cwm Bychan and Cwm Nantcol are often thought of as twin valleys, they each have an entirely different character. The dramatic precipices and gnarled oak woods of Cwm Bychan are replaced in Cwm Nantcol by a more open and gentle landscape, with well cultivated land in the valley bottom divided by a sparkling river. Certainly, if one arrives in the valley by way of the Drws Ardudwy, one feels a certain lifting of the spirits as Mr. Bingley mentions: 'After this dreary scene, we entered a more wide and fertile valley, called Cwm Nantcol, the hollow of the sunken brook, ...'

That the early tourists hardly mention this valley is perhaps indicative of the degree to which it has remained unchanged over the centuries. If it was just ordinary farm land to them, and not worthy of special comment, then the fact that it is un-altered today makes it of particular interest to the modern tourist. With the grassy dome of Moelfre to the south, Mynydd Llanbedr and Foel Wen's rounded shoulders rising in a series of small pastures

Cwm Nantcol

and open sheep walks to the north, and the darker bulk of the two Rhinog peaks separated by the deep cleft of the Drws Ardudwy standing sentinel in the east, this is a world apart. Here one can spend days exploring a multitude of paths, always with a new prospect before you.

One of the best times to see Cwm Nantcol is on a fine summer evening, when this west facing valley is flooded with the warm light of the setting sun. The old farm buildings glow among green meadows, with Cardigan Bay a blue-mauve ribbon in the distance.

An ideal viewing point can be found if you take a steep track which is sign-posted from the road by Pont Cerrig, the last bridge over the river before you reach Maesygarnedd. This was built to serve mine workings high on Foel Wen. Follow it for about 20 minutes until the gradient eases, when you will reach a place where you can look out over the whole of the valley and far beyond; a truly pre-industrial landscape of farms and small fields.

One beautiful summer evening I brought two young Canadian students to this spot; they were only in the country for a day or so and wanted to feel that they had seen the real Wales. It seemed to me that this view epitomised the ancient landscape which is typical of Ardudwy, and would be quite different from anything which they would have experienced at home. Like me they have family connections with North Wales, and I suppose that I also wanted them to experience their heritage, and know what it would have been like to live in these hills when their forefathers were alive. I pompously explained that five centuries ago this valley had probably looked much the same as it does today, and sat back in my comfortable bed of heather, warmed by the gentle evening sun, waiting for them to enthuse. They didn't! Of course I had the 'time-scale' all wrong. Had I said 'one hundred years ago', no doubt I could have revelled in their 'Oos'! and 'Ahhs'!, but half a millenium ago, when hill farming was already an ancient occupation here, and Colonel John Jones's parents lived at Maesygarnedd far below us, Columbus had not long since set foot on the continent which is their homeland. I might as well have been talking in terms of geological time.

The seashore is a constant, occasionally glimpsed, presence while in the mountains, and it is worth remembering that even on days when the valleys are grey with rain and the summits hidden by cloud, it is often clear and sunny only a few miles to the west. From the summit of Rhinog Fawr to the beach at Mochras is only about six miles(9.5 km), but in that distance the rainfall gradient drops from an average of 80 ins. (2000 mm) per annum to 40 ins. (1000 mm).

When you return from the mountains to Llanbedr village, you will find a road which runs down along the riverside beyond the bridge, and this will take you to Mochras, which is also known as Shell Island. It is no longer an island in the precise sense of the word, for it is not completely surrounded by water, but its atmosphere is still very much that of an island. After passing the airfield, a modern tarmacked causeway will bring you safely across the sands of the estuary to the Shell Island Reception Centre. This road is only closed at high spring tides, and a notice board gives warning of when this is likely to be.

Before the new harbour was created at Pensarn, the river flowed south past the meadows where the airfield now stands, and reached the sea about half a mile south of the ancient farmhouse which, then as now, dominates the skyline. Another channel, following the same course as the river does today, entered the bay at the north end of Mochras. It is said that the island's Welsh name, which can be translated as 'Pig Race', derives from the sight of the pigs which were bred there fleeing across the sands, pursued by the rising tide. Its other name, 'Shell Island', exactly describes one of its main features, and it is for the shells, and the miles of sandy beaches backed by a wilderness of sandhills, that people come here. These beaches are so vast that even at the height of the summer you need only walk a little way from the main car park to find peace and seclusion.

The quantities of shells on the beach vary from season to season and year to year, but there are nearly always some interesting ones to see, and usually the number and variety are astonishing. If casually picking up a few shells is part of any trip to the beach today, earlier generations of tourists had a rather more serious minded attitude to such recreations, as an article in Mr. Askew Robert's *Gossiping Guide to Wales* illustrates.

CONCHOLOGY IN NORTH WALES
by
The Rev. Carleton Greene

How many there are who find the sea-side dull for want of occupation! To all such let me recommend the childish recreation of collecting shells. Without advancing far into the mysteries and difficulties of the science of Conchology, enough may be known to give zest to sea-side rambles and to supply a healthy and pure excitement much needed in hours of idleness.

The lover of shells ..... may explore the coast in the neighbourhood of Harlech and return laden with spoils. The chief object to be aimed at is to reach Mochras Island at the right state of the tide, and to spend as long a time as he can.

The Harlech beach itself, though very fine, is not favourable to the conchologist. There is one shell, however, *Lutaria elliptica,* which is easily broken, and is better sought on the smooth sand of Harlech than amongst the rocks of Mochras.

At Mochras you walk ankle-deep in shells, and every wave, as the tide comes up, dashes fresh treasures at your feet.

In spite of his fear that the devil would find work for idle hands, unless they are employed in picking up shells, his enthusiasm for this subject is infectious. It is surprising how many hours one can spend, even on a day when the wind is cold, lying full length in the shelter of a rock just sifting through the material within reach, perfectly content even if, like the author, you only know the names of some of the more abundant varieties. Stones may be associated with discomfort, but one soon discovers that sea-rounded pebbles of the right grade can be just as comfortable as a bean-bag. If you are in a group, then this can quickly turn into a fairly competitive activity. When the time comes to move on, it is worth calling in at the Shell Island Reception Centre, where a very comprehensive collection of shells made by the owner's daughter is displayed in a glass case. In an appendix at the end of this book you will also find the Reverend Carleton Greene's list of shells found on Mochras and Harlech beaches. Even if, at first sight, the Latin names look rather daunting, it is reassuring to know that many of the shells listed have common names; Pelican's Foot, Barrel Shell, Elephant's Tusk, Sailor's Button, the mysterious Cowrie and many others. For those who wish to identify their 'finds', many of the bookshops in the area sell simple guides to the sea-shore.

The farmhouse on Mochras was the home of one of Wales's great poets, the bard Sion Phylip (1543? - 1620), a member of the famous dynasty of poets which flourished in Ardudwy during the sixteenth and seventeenth centuries. He was a prolific author of poems written according to the strict metre of traditional Welsh forms: *cywyddau, awdlau* and *englynion*. In February 1620 he was drowned while returning by boat from Pwllheli to Mochras, after completing a bardic tour of Anglesey and Caernarfonshire. He is buried by the east window of Llandanwg Church, on the other side of the estuary.

Before returning to Llanbedr again it is worth mentioning the railway line which you cross at what used to be called Talwrn Bach halt, which has now been rather prosaically re-named Llanbedr Station although it is some distance from the village. The Cambrian Coast Line, from Pwllheli on the Llŷn Peninsula to Machynlleth, is one of those rare railways which is worth travelling on just for the sake of what you will see out of the window. Walkers also find it useful, as it makes many longer excursions possible by forming a useful link between where you start and where you finish.

Crossing the bridge over the Artro once again, we are now only four miles from Harlech by the main road, but before reaching this historic town it is worth making one more brief detour, to visit Llandanwg. If you turn left when you reach the village of Llanfair and drive down-hill towards the sea, with the estuary and Mochras spread out before you, you will find a large car park behind the beach. The sea-shore here has a quite different feel from Mochras; rockier, with smaller sand-hills, and a more sheltered aspect. Shells are not quite so abundant as they are on the other side of the estuary, but a fine collection displayed in the excellent Maes Cafe beside the car park shows what can be found.

In the days of the early tourists the transition from the hurly burly of the main coast road to this quiet backwater was less abrupt than it is for motorists now. In 1800 Richard Fenton rode across the water meadows from Llanbedr to visit one of the oldest churches in Wales.

From here, leaving Cae Nest to the right, the old Seat of the Pooles, cross another Bridge, under which runs a River that joins the Artro a little below, making one Estuary. Cross over part of a Marsh, for the enclosing of which a late Act was passed, to Llandanwg, a church situated on the Beach, and by having its chief Door towards the sea, filled with Sand. The building simple and old. The East Window, and two side ones of the Chancel were of free stone and had been handsomely wrought. In the Chancel two Monuments, one a handsome mural Marble Monument to a Gentleman of the name of Edwards, of Tregayan, in Anglesey, and who had been of Oriel Coll : Oxon, and was drowned with 3 others crossing to Cricciaeth, A.D. 1753. Another consisting of Escutcheons cut in oak at the Back of a Pew, to some of the family of Wynnes of Las Ynis. Chancel separated from Nave by a neat old carved oak screen. Enquired for any tomb in the Church that I could find out Sir R. Thimbleby, but in vain. However, the Clerk shewed me a Tomb originally raised with Mason Work about a Foot above the surface, covered with an uninscribed course flag, and said there were letters on the site; so getting a spade, we removed the sward that had grown so as to entirely hide the sides, and found one square piece of Freestone inscribed, which I make no doubt of being the tomb of the Knight Speed speaks of, whose tomb in this time might have been well known and explained by those who shewed it. The Clerk likewise said that it was not claimed by any family in the Parish, and therefore must have belonged to a Stranger, as every one of the other tombs was known.

The Shells on this Coast are very small, but very beautiful and very various. There are Sand Eels, Prawns, Lobsters, and Oysters taken hereabouts.

This church has been a place of worship for over 1500 years, and was probably founded by Irish monks who crossed the sea in hide-covered curraghs to convert the Welsh tribes to Christianity. It is dedicated to Saint Tanwg, a somewhat shadowy figure in the history of the Celtic Church, of whom little is known. The very setting and character of the building evokes that distant time, when courageous seafaring evangelists were establishing a toe-hold along this treacherous coast. With the Irish Sea behind them and the prospect of hostility from the people who surrounded their outposts of faith, it is hard to overestimate the dedication and courage of these hardy monks.

Wandering among the grave stones, only a few of which have been revealed by the shifting sand, one is constantly aware of the antiquity of this place. The simple white-washed interior of the church brings a feeling of peace which only a timeless tradition of worship seems to inspire. Until the 1830's this was the parish

The lychgate, Llandanwg

church of Harlech, and no-one knows how many more graves lie under the protective blanket of sandhills. Services are still held here, regularly during the summer and intermittently during the winter, when the church is lit by candles and oil lamps. Details of these services can be found on the notice board beside the lych gate.

138

If you return to the main road, and turn left towards Harlech, you will immediately be confronted by one of the most famous views in Wales. Here the whole of the bay which is enclosed by the Llŷn Peninsula, together with the full sweep of Harlech beach, the Traethau Bychan and Mawr with Snowdon rising in the distance, will be spread out before you. This is appropriately known as 'surprise corner', partly because of the dramatic suddenness with which the view comes into sight, but also because in the days when the road was narrower at this point drivers were often distracted by the view, heedless of oncoming traffic.

In 1799 Sir Robert Ker Porter, fresh from the delights of watching the bathers on Barmouth beach, approached Harlech from this direction, but not by the road which we use today as this was constructed relatively recently. The old road was higher up the hillside, and still exists as a narrow by-way between Llanfair and Harlech, so he saw this wonderful prospect from a slightly different angle.

> Left Barmouth on the 19th. for Harlech. The road to the left for the whole way is flanked by the sea, on the right, by bare uninteresting and rocky heights. There is no view of any consequence until within a mile and a half of Harlech, when a vast and infinite collection of mountains present themselves, Snowdon high above this mob of earthly warts, veiled thick in sable atmosphere. The sea rolls into a sort of large bay at their foot, and on a high rocky promontory in the foreground rose the castle of Harlech an ancient and splendid Radcliffian creation.

This unforgettable panorama has lost nothing with the passing of the years, and may still be the best free entertainment in Ardudwy.

CHAPTER 5

HARLECH AND ITS CASTLE

The main gate, Harlech Castle

Castles and tourists seem to have a natural affinity with each other, and few of us wonder why travelling for pleasure should include scrutiny of such sinister instruments of destruction. However mellow the stonework of their walls or picturesque their dilapidation may be, the object of any castle's builders was quite single-minded; to assist in the waging of war. Because such places were designed to withstand the onslaughts of armies, their great strength has also served them well in the battle against the depredations of time, so that many have survived almost unscathed through the centuries. Together with churches, and particularly cathedrals, they represent the oldest structures which tourists commonly encounter, but they lack the intimacy of the former or the outstanding beauty of many of the latter. Perhaps the most optimistic explanation of our fascination with them is that they are often associated with heroism, for there is virtue in putting the common cause before personal preservation, but that common cause is still likely to involve killing, maiming and laying waste.

A castle should not really be a cheerful place to visit, and yet when we go on holiday we flock to them in our thousands, which is fortunate for the Welsh tourist industry, as Wales has a remarkable number of them. Among these are fourteen which were built some six hundred years ago by Edward I as a chain of garrisons which extend from Caernarfon and Conwy on the north coast as far as Builth in the south; Harlech being one of the finest among them. They are the visible proof of the determination of one English monarch, who was prepared to use the latest technology, and recruit the premier military engineers of the day from the continent of Europe, to maintain the integrity of his kingdom. If when visiting cathedrals we prefer to forget that they act as repositories for human remains, then when visiting these castles it is perhaps understandable to overlook their purpose of intimidating and subjugating the people of this ancient country.

The early tourists reached Harlech either by following the coast road, with a stop at Barmouth, or if they were in a hurry, by making a day-trip from Tan-y-bwlch. Even at the end of the eighteenth century this was one of the places which any visitor to Wales would want to see, but its fame was entirely due to the castle. The town itself held no attraction, and G. N. Wright in his *Scenes in North Wales*, published in 1833, describes the place in terms which are no more dismissive than those of many other authors.

Harlech, now a poor village, deriving its tenure in the memory of travellers from a noble castle, was formerly the capital of the county, and erected into a free borough by King Edward the First. But the great sessions have been removed to Dolgelly and Bala, and the privilege of sending a burgess to parliament was forfeited by neglect. The corporation consists of a mayor, recorder, bailiffs and burgesses, and their register is now in possession of a blacksmith in the village. The charter was stolen by the captain of a merchant vessel, who desired to see the authority upon which he was required to pay toll at Gest Point; when the ancient deed was put in his hand, he dishonestly and villainously refused to return it, and put out to sea. Ormsby Gore of Porkington Esq., the representative of the house of Cleneny, has restored the little county hall, in which the member for Merionethshire continues to be elected, and at other times it is appropriated to the charitable purpose of a poor school.

Earlier in the century, in about 1722, Daniel Defoe, travelling in his capacity as a government agent (the eighteenth century equivalent of a secret policeman), passed through Harlech and has left us this bleak reference to his visit.

There are but few large towns in all this part nor is it very populous; indeed much of it is scarce habitable but, 'tis said, there are more sheep in it than in all the rest of Wales. On the sea shore however, we see Harleigh Castle, which is still a garrison, and kept for the guard of the coast but 'tis of no great strength, but by its situation.

This was written just prior to the industrial revolution, and immediately following a long period of civil unrest. With the declining strategic importance of this stronghold, the legal and administrative business of the county passed to the rising commercial centres of Dolgellau and Bala. Harlech experienced a period of decline which would only end when tourism brought a new wave of prosperity in the mid-nineteenth century. Today it is a popular local shopping centre, with an air of antiquity fostered by its stone houses ranging over the steep hillside, and a charming narrow main street. Its situation, high above the coastal plain, provides tantalising glimpses of sea and mountains between the houses.

When approaching from the south, the castle is hidden until you are quite close to it, but from the north its sinister bulk is visible for many miles across the flat expanse of the morfa. This dramatic silhouette on a distant skyline has become one of the icons of Welsh landscape painting and photography. It was from this direction that many of the early tourists came, and they had a choice of route, either hiring a guide to cross the sands of the Traeth Bychan which were considered to be dangerous, or following a 'road' over the shoulders of the hills which included staircase paths. G. N. Wright, in his *Scenes in North Wales*, indicates how remote Harlech was considered to be before the turnpikes were built.

> A few years back even tourists were content with the history of Harlech, particularly if it happened to be accompanied by an illustration of the fine castle. The singular ruggedness of the way, and the wretchedness of the lodgings, threw a damp on the ardour of even the most inquisitive. These objections are happily no longer applicable, a new road is formed between Maes y Neuadd and Glyn, and Sir Robert Vaughan has erected a spacious and handsome inn at Harlech, where admirable accommodations are afforded upon singularly moderate terms.

Harriet Alderson, a well-to-do lady from the Midlands who was travelling with a large party including servants, provides a graphic description of what it was like to make a journey by coach on the old road. While they were preparing to leave Harlech they were given some warning of what was in store for them:

> ......the post boy came to us and insisted on putting the four horses to the phaeton, saying that he could not possibly get over

the next stage without. For sometime we resisted the measure, the carriage being so extremely light, but the man was so earnest that we were obliged to give way and soon found he was perfectly right. The first part of the road was through very deep sand, afterwards ascending almost perpendicular slate rocks. At times it was with the greatest difficulty the phaeton, with only one person in it, could get along.

Later in the day, when they were descending to Maentwrog, the whole party had to walk as the post boy 'could not answer for our safety if we remained in the carriage.'

Only the energetic and resourceful Mr Roscoe managed to avoid any inconvenience in reaching Harlech, but then he was a professional travel writer.

> Taking a boat near Criceath, I had a pleasant sail through part of Cardigan Bay to Harlech. This mean little town, now only remarkable for its feudal castle, was formerly a place of considerable importance, and a fortified post of the Romans and Britons, defending the openings of the two Traeths, and securing a communication with the opposite shore.

Having reached the town, few of the early tourists would have been disappointed by its castle. This immense structure, together with Dolwyddelan, Cricieth and Castell y Bere, was intended to help subjugate Ardudwy after Llywelyn the Great's uprising. It is still essentially the same structure which Edward I commissioned, and unlike some of the others with which his name is associated, it is not an existing Welsh structure which he captured and then rebuilt. For the present day visitor it has the merit of having survived in a form which is more faithful to its original construction than many of the others, having escaped extensive alteration and re-building. Its situation is certainly more dramatic than any of its rivals. Most of the tourists seem to have taken their descriptions of its origin and history straight out of Pennant's *Tour in Wales*, but then that meticulous scholar would have provided all the information which was currently available. Fortunately it is not necessary to be a historian to enjoy Harlech Castle. For those who are put off by ancient monuments, and have difficulty distinguishing between Edward IV and Henry VIII, a walk round the battlements is still an exciting and unforgettable experience. As G. N. Wright says:

> No view in the north shires, is superior to the prospect from the light turrets of Harlech Castle. The Marsh and Traeth are seen spread out at a frightful depth, and from the margins of their wide level, stupendous rocks and cliffs suddenly start up, tufted and embossed with wood. A great mass of air seems to float in the void behind the scene, separating a world of mountains, the grandeur of whose features only the pencil can express. A stupendous vista of broken hills forms a noble perspective, crossed by ranges that open to further glimpses —- summit succeeds to summit in endless train, leading the fancy into regions of solitary obscurity.

For anyone looking at the massive stonework of the curtain walls, and speculating on the immense labour required to bring the necessary materials to this remote site, it is hard not to be curious about its origins. *Lewis's Topographical Dictionary of Wales*, first published in 1833, also provides a version of the castle's history which would have been generally accepted at the time of the early tourists.

> It is evident that it was formerly a fortified post of the ancient Britons, and was called Twr Bronwen, from Bronwen, the sister of Bran ab Llŷr, Prince of Siluria or Gwent. It afterwards obtained the name of Caer Collwyn, from having been, towards the close of the ninth century, the residence of Collwyn ab Tango, a chieftain of one of the fifteen tribes of North Wales, and lord of Eivionydd, Ardudwy, and part of Lleyn, who inhabited a square tower which

subsequently became a portion of the more modern castle, and of which there are yet some remains. According to some of the British historians, the castle was founded, so early as the year 530, by Maelgwyn Gwynedd, Prince of North Wales: the present structure was built by Edward I, upon the ruins of the former, and was called Arlech, from its situation upon the rock, or by its present name of Harlech, which signifies "the fair rock:" it was completed prior to the year 1283, for at that time Hugh de Wlonkeslow was constable, with a small garrison under him, and had an allowance of £100 per annum, which, however, was afterwards much reduced.

Modern scholars tell a rather less romantic story, for archaeologists have been unable to find any trace of an earlier building on this site, but if you visit the castle you will find the most recent version of its history displayed near the entrance. Among the greatest delights of Harlech is that it is one of those magical places where history and legend meet. Scientific research serves us well enough in building up a record of its past, as far back as the thirteenth century at least, but beyond

A by-way, Harlech

that we are in the indistinct regions of the dark ages, and must rely on oral tradition. For the origins of the castle are bound up with the birth of Celtic culture and we only have access to this part of its history through the collection of tales known as the

Mabinogion. Probably first written down by scribes in the fourteenth century, these sagas date from a much earlier period, and may reach back to the shadowy times before recorded history. There are four main sections of the Mabinogion, and it is the one recounting the tragedy of Branwen the Fair that concerns us, for it gives substance to the belief that Twr Branwen occupied this site before the present castle was built.

The legend tells us that one day long, long ago, Bendigeidfran, King of the Land of the Mighty, was seated with his family and courtiers on the rocks where the castle now stands, looking out over the sea. Among the company were his brother Manawydan son of Llŷr, and also his half brothers on his mother's side, Nisien and Efnisien, two men of character. Nisien was a man of peace, always eager to promote harmony, but Efnisien loved conflict and looked for ways to create hostility and strife.

They were watching thirteen boats approaching from the direction of Ireland, and the king ordered his men to arm themselves and wait by the shore, for these were troubled times. As the strangers approached Harlech beach, a shield was raised in one of the boats, held up-side-down to indicate that the occupants mission was peaceful. Matholwch, King of Ireland, had come to ask for the hand of Branwen, the beautiful daughter of Llŷr, in order to seal an alliance between his and Bendigeidfran's kingdoms. It was agreeable to the king to give his sister in marriage to Matholwch, so he invited the party to land, but they declined and it was agreed that they should sail on to Aberffraw on Anglesey were the marriage would take place. Some time later, both courts assembled in a city of tents erected round this beautiful bay. Branwen and Matholwch were married, with all the ceremony and feasting which such a majestic occasion required.

Efnisien saw an opportunity to create trouble. Claiming that he had not been consulted about the marriage of his sister, he took revenge on the Irish court by mutilating their horses when he found them unattended one day. He cut off their ears, their lips, their eyelids and their tails.

When Matholwch heard what had happened, he and his company immediately left the camp and prepared to return to Ireland, but Bendigeidfran sent emissaries after them, offering compensation in the form of horses and a magic cauldron which could be used to restore to life warriors who had fallen in battle. Though Matholwch felt the insult which he had suffered acutely, he eventually agreed to return, and the celebrations continued, but in an atmosphere of suspicion and mistrust. Gradually good relations between the two courts were restored, so that by the time Matholwch and Branwen set sail for Ireland all seemed to be well.

The first year of Branwen's marriage was happy, and she bore Matholwch a son whom they named Gwern. By distributing much of the treasure which she had brought with her from Wales among the Irish courtiers, she became popular. But the insult which the king had suffered at the hands of the Welsh was not forgotten; a powerful faction was still hostile to Branwen. They took their revenge by isolating her from her husband and forcing her to work as a skivvy in the kitchens, instructing the butcher to beat her at the end of each day. Matholwch feared that news of this mistreatment of his queen would reach Wales, so he forbade any of his ships to sail there, and imprisoned any travellers who reached Irish shores from that country.

In her misery Branwen had befriended a starling which came to perch on the rim of the trough in which she kneaded dough. By kindness and patience she taught the bird to speak, and concealing a letter describing her husband's brutality under its wing, told it to fly to Wales and find Bendigeidfran. One day the starling alighted on the Welsh king's shoulder while he was presiding over an assembly at Caer Seint in Arfon. He immediately raised a great army to invade Ireland.

When he landed, the Irish were so impressed by Bendigeidfran's mighty stature, and by his ability to use magic powers to assist him in battle, that they insisted that Matholwch should make peace. Envoys were sent to propose that, in return for Bendigeidfran's forgiveness, Matholwch would make Gwern, Branwen's son, King of Ireland. A meeting of both armies was arranged in a vast hut built specially for the occasion. It was lit by hundreds of flaring torches, with a huge fire burning in the middle of the floor around which the leaders sat. Among them was the trouble-maker Efnisien. When Gwern was presented to Bendigeidfran he accepted the Irish proposal immediately, as did Manawydan and Nisien. But when Gwern stood before Efnisien, that evil man grasped the child by the heels and threw him into the fire. The fighting which followed this contemptible act left the flower of both nations dead, and Bendigeidfran mortally wounded by a poisoned spear. The dying King commanded that his head should be cut off and taken to London, where it could be buried facing France. After the carnage in the hut only seven of the invaders and the unfortunate Branwen remained to carry out his wishes. The Irish had attempted to use the magic cauldron to restore their own warriors to life, but Efnisien had managed to smash it, thus preventing their regeneration and his own.

The small party bearing Bendigeidfran's head set off to carry out his last wishes, and when they reached Aber Alaw, in Anglesey, they stopped to rest. There Branwen's heart broke. With a great sigh she said 'Alas, Son of God, woe is me that ever I was born: two good islands have been wasted because of me!' She died there and was buried.

This bitter tale of betrayal and casual violence clearly reaches back into the dark ages after the Roman Legions had left Britain, and possibly far, far beyond. Even if archaeologists have been unable to find any trace of an earlier structure on the site of Edward I's great castle, the legend associated with Twr Branwen lives on. In 1813 a cist was excavated on Anglesey at the place where, according to the Mabinogion, Branwen had been buried. It was constructed in the rectangular form which the Mabinogion describes as her last resting place. There was great excitement when the remains of a young woman, probably of royal birth, were found inside this tomb; but sadly we are told that the grave belongs to a later period than that of Branwen the Fair.

Harlech castle has always had a close association with the Welsh nationalist movement. Originally built as a symbol of English power in Wales, it became an obvious target, together with Edward's other castles, for anyone wishing to re-establish Wales as an independent nation. In the year 1399 the enigmatic Owain Glyndŵr became the leader of a movement which nearly succeeded.

There is little in Owain's background to explain why he should have taken up arms so readily, indeed he had shown every sign of being a conformist in his early life. But he displayed a remarkable talent for guerilla warfare when, in middle life, he raised his standard in a cause which sought to restore the autonomy of the Welsh nation which had been lost at the time of the Norman invasion of Britain. The early tourists do not dwell on this aspect of Anglo-Welsh relations. Perhaps this is out of delicacy, but more probably it is because little more than half a century after a Scots army had invaded the north of England, marching as far south as Derby, and while a considerable army of occupation was required in Ireland, the unity of the British Isles was still a major political issue. Indeed only a year before the Reverend William Bingley visited Harlech, a French expeditionary force had landed in Pembrokeshire, admittedly by accident and with results which were more farcical than threatening, in the hope of raising the Welsh in a crusade against England on behalf of Napoleon. In 1798 Bingley only gives the bare bones of Owain Glyndŵr's exploits at Harlech.

> In the year 1404, this Castle, along with that of Aberystwyth, in Cardiganshire, was seized by the great, but ambitious Owen Glyndŵr, during his rebellion against Henry IV. They were both taken about four years afterwards, by an army which the king had despatched to Wales, against that sturdy chieftain.

At the age of forty this scion of a wealthy and influential family, with considerable estates on the borders of Wales, had a typical career for his time behind him, and might have been expected to be contemplating the prospect of a secure old age. He had been educated in the law at Westminster, seen military action in the service of the crown in Scotland in 1385, and had

The castle from lower Harlech

151

an income from his lands alone of over £100 per annum, a considerable sum at that time. By 1400 all this had changed.

A dispute over land, not remarkable during this turbulent period in the Welsh Marches, escalated when a gathering of Marcher Barons declared Owain Glyndŵr the rightful heir to the Princes of Wales. By moving his forces rapidly, Henry IV was able to check the progress of this revolt without undue trouble, and on the surface that seemed to be the end of the matter. But Henry was not secure in his possession of the throne of England, and he enacted punitive legislation against the Welsh, thus providing the motivation for a far more serious uprising which quickly spread to the whole of Wales. By 1401 Owain Glyndŵr had the support not only of the Welsh landowners, but also of young, English educated Welshmen, who could provide him with the administrative skills needed to consolidate his military successes. By providing effective Government of the parts of the country he controlled, and particularly by instituting a legal system based on traditional Welsh law, he became far more than a successful military leader. Six years after the start of his revolt he was in a position to call parliaments of his supporters, one of which may have been held at Harlech. His influence extended throughout most of the principality, and at last it seemed possible that Wales would establish itself as an independent sovereign state. This was not to be. A military expedition into England ended in confusion and retreat, and the impetus of the uprising was lost. Harlech Castle was besieged by the forces of the King in 1408, and when it fell in 1409 Owain Glyndŵr lost not only one of his most important strategic assets, but also his family, who were captured along with much of his wealth. By 1410 he was a fugitive.

Had he been no more than a gifted guerilla leader, his reputation might not occupy the exalted position in the pantheon of Welsh heroes which it does today. But Owain

Glyndŵr looked far beyond the immediate preoccupation of military success to the establishment of a civil administration which gave Welshmen a glimpse of what an independent Wales could be like. This vision has never faded and still fuels the nationalist movement today. In a country where romance is a major component of patriotism, the end of Owain's career consolidated his reputation for all time. Had he been captured and executed he would have become a martyr in the cause of freedom; one among many. However he was not captured, but simply vanished among the hills, and history does not record when or how he met his end. This has given his spirit immortality; for many Welshmen this chapter of their history has never been closed.

The end of the Glyndŵr revolt brought an uneasy peace to Wales, for a time at least, but this was a century of constant strife, and before its end Harlech was to enter the history books again, as an important stronghold of the Lancastrians during the Wars of the Roses. A dramatic account of its eventual capture is given by the Reverend John Evans in 1798.

This, like other fortresses, has witnessed many tempestuous scenes, and been frequently subject to a variety of masters. During the civil wars, between the Houses of York and Lancaster, Daffydd ap Jenkin ap Einion, a British nobleman siding with the House of Lancaster, defended his castle nobly against Edward the Fourth, till William Herbert, Earl of Pembroke, forcing his way through the Alps of Snowdon, (a passage deemed impracticable) at length invested a place before considered as impregnable. Pembroke committed the siege to his brother Sir Richard, who sent a menacing summons to the British Commandant. Dafydd returned an answer becoming a man of such distinguished merit: He had "kept a castle so long in France, that he had made all the old women of France talk of him: and he was determined to keep this so long, that all the old women in England should talk of him." He was however obliged by famine to surrender: but upon terms so honourable, as his defence was obstinate. Richard stipulated to save his life, by interceding with the King; but Edward indignantly refused: when Pembroke stepping up, told him plainly, that he might take his life instead of the brave commander's, or he would assuredly replace Dafydd in his Castle, and his Majesty might send whom he pleased to take him out again.

Henry Penruddocke Wyndham adds this chilling poem to his account of the same incident, for though Pembroke may have dealt honourably with Dafydd ap Ienkin, his military expedition through North Wales was a brutally punitive one.

Sir John Wynne, in his history of the Gwedir family, quotes the following British lines, on the ravages which were committed by him [Pembroke], through the countries of Merioneth and Denbeigh.

> Harlech a Dinbech, pob dôr — yn cynnau,
> Nanconwy yn farwor,
> Mil a phedwarcant i'm Iôr,
> A thrugain ag wyth rhagor.

At Harlech and Denbeigh every house was in flames, and Nanconway in cinders; one thousand and four hundred from our Lord, and sixty eight more.

Towards the end of this civil war, one of England's most colourful Queens came to the castle. The Reverend John Evans again.

Margaret of Anjou, the spirited queen of Henry the sixth, after having escaped the grasp of Lord Stanley, subsequent to the King's defeat at Northampton, found in this fortress an asylum from her pursuers; till being invited by her adherents in Scotland, she was able to take the field, and near Wakefield defeat the enemy, and destroy the leader.

With its turbulent history of revolt against the confines of English rule, it is surprising to find that the castle's final moment of glory was to be as the last Royalist stronghold in Wales to fall to Oliver Cromwell during the Civil War.

When you enter the inner ward of the castle through the narrow gate-passage, once protected by no fewer than three portcullis, you emerge into a vast open space dominated by the graceful lines of the gate-house. This is not just an example of military engineering, but a structure of real architectural merit; as pleasing to the eye as it is impressive. Even those who know the castle well from the outside cannot fail to be surprised by the interior, for there is a peaceful, almost domestic atmosphere within which is in sharp contrast to the rather brutal impression given by its exterior. Exploring the numerous towers, passages and staircases it is natural to see this inner core in terms of the everyday lives of the people who lived here. For between episodes of warfare there were long periods of peace, when Harlech served as a garrison. Within the courtyard one is totally immersed in the atmosphere of another age, when even a purely functional building like this one was created with a regard for aesthetics which seems largely to have been lost in our own time. As you pass through the doorway, which once connected the great hall with the outer ward, you emerge from the confines of the curtain walls onto the manicured lawns of a wide terrace, only to be confronted by a spectacle in the foreground of which no-one can be proud.

This is a planner's nightmare, with urban sprawl lapping up to the very base of the castle cliff, where once an inlet of the Irish sea provided a harbour by which the garrison could be supplied. Fortunately if you sit on one of the benches thoughtfully provided in the shelter of the ramparts, all this disappears beneath the parapet of the outer wall, and one is looking at a wild and beautiful prospect of sandhills, sea and hills. The peaceful spell cast by the inner courtyard is instantly restored.

This is as pleasant a place to while away a few minutes as you will find in Ardudwy, and perhaps to compare the age of the Castle's builders with that of the early tourists, and with the one in which we now live. While looking out over the bay you may see a military aircraft making its final approach to land at the Royal Aircraft Establishment at Llanbedr; a graphic example of how war has changed during the seven hundred years since the castle was built. Unfortunately its effect on ordinary people has not changed at all.

The care and sensitivity with which the castle is maintained by Cadw: Welsh Historic Monuments, makes it a joy to visit, but in the days of the early tourists there was no such organisation, and visitors had to fend for themselves, as Catherine Sinclair discovered in the 1830s. She was an aristocratic Scot who spent the early part of her life as political secretary to her father, and devoted her later years to writing and good works. Of a rigidly Calvinistic turn of mind, she was not entirely without a sense of humour.

> The principal staircase here had entirely fallen down, which I was not perfectly inconsolable to perceive, because in every ruin there generally is a narrow tottering ascent, scarcely practicable, and quite in the dark, which tourists are expected to scramble up at all hazards. If the stairs of every ancient keep-tower I have mounted in my time could be piled one above another, they would go a considerable way towards the moon. A——— at last succeeded in rummaging out what he considered to be a tolerable flight of steps; indeed, he cares so little to encounter a mile of ruinous perpendicular stairs, that if he passed a day on the tread-mill it would apparently be a sort of rest to him. I was on the point of

yielding to my fate, and took 'le premiere pas', when the guide unexpectedly interposed, declaring, that though 'some gentlemen of great steadiness had been known to reach the summit of that tower in safety, he never could scale it himself, and dared not now accompany us on the enterprise.' This very rational view of the subject appeared so convincing, that I gladly retraced the three steps I had already mounted, while A——— unflinchingly proceeded to escalade the castle with a degree of steadiness which an engineer might emulate, and soon emerged on the highest pinnacle of the crumbling battlement, whence he probably saw a very extended horizon of sea.

A guide is no longer necessary when visiting the castle, and the staircases, though still steep and uneven in places, are not dangerous. One of the rooms leading off the gate-house passage houses an exhibition which provides a well presented introduction to the castle's history, and this can be supplemented with books and pamphlets which are on sale at the entrance.

Though most of the early tourists have left rather earnest descriptions of their visits, there is one exception. Joseph Hucks was studying law at the time of his tour, and he published his journal in 1795. It is remarkable for the fact that, although he never identifies his companions, we now know that one of them was Samuel Taylor Coleridge, a fellow student at Cambridge.

We ..... also here achieved an exploit, which, beyond all doubt, gives us some title to military prowess; for as there did not happen to be anyone in the way, who might open the gates of the castle, and our time not permitting us to wait for the ordinary forms of capitulation, we boldly marched up to the assault, and scaling the walls at four different places, took possession of the garrison, as it were by 'coup de main.' But for this daring outrage, we would well nigh have got into an awkward scrape; some of the inhabitants observing our operations, and probably taking us for free-booters, gave the alarm; and mustering a formidable body of forces, marched in military array, to dispossess us of our stronghold. But we soon pacified our opponents, and having convinced them that our intentions were neither predatory nor hostile, they retired to an ale-house to banish sorrow, and indulged themselves, at our expense, in copious libations of ale.

If we owe our knowledge of Twr Branwen to legend, and that of Edward I's castle to history, there is also a phenomenon associated with Harlech which seems to have its origins in rumour. This is a very strange story indeed, as the Reverend William Bingley recounts.

In the winter of 1694, this neighbourhood was much alarmed by a kind of kindled exhalation, which came from a sandy marshy tract of land, called Morfa Bychan, across the channel, eight miles towards Harlech, and injured much of the country, by poisoning the grass in such a manner as to kill the cattle, and firing hay and corn ricks for near a mile from the coast. It is represented to have had the appearance of a weak blue flame, which, by any great noise, such as the firing of guns, or the sounding of horns, was easily extinguished. All the damage was done invariably at night, and in the course of the winter not less than sixteen hay ricks and two barns, one filled with corn, and the other with hay, were burned by it. It did not seem to affect anything else, and men could go into it without receiving the least injury. It is said, that though it was seen oftener during the first three weeks than it was afterwards, yet it was observed at different intervals of time for at least eight months. The occasion of this singular phenomenon is not exactly known. It appears most probably to have arisen from some collections of putrid substances, the vapour coming from which might have been directed towards this place by the wind. Bishop Gibson has conjectured, that it might have proceeded from the corrupted bodies of a quantity of locusts, which came into the kingdom about that time, but from the coldness of the climate were destroyed. He says, that a considerable quantity of them were seen lying dead about the shores of Aberdaron, in Caernarvonshire.

Most of the early tourists mention this incident, and all their accounts seem to tally with that given in Edmund Gibson's revised and enlarged edition of *Camden's Britannia*, published in 1722, so their interest may owe more to their knowledge of this passage than to any information gathered during their visits. If there was further information available around Harlech, in the form of oral history, then it escaped even those diligent Welsh speaking authors Richard Fenton and Thomas Pennant. Such a phenomenon could possibly be caused by a build-up of methane gas, produced by rotting organic material, and it is not unusual for vast quantities of seaweed to be deposited on the beaches after violent winter storms. However examination of Gibson's work reveals that his account relies entirely on letters from one informant.

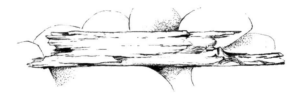

Driftwood on Harlech Beach

No visit to Harlech can be complete without seeing its remarkable beach, which runs in an elegant and unbroken curve from a point just south of the town, for nearly four miles northwards. With its barrier of dunes separating it from the coastal plain, and the hills of the Llŷn Peninsula leading the eye steadily westward to the limitless horizon of the Irish Sea, it is as fine a place for walking as it is for sun-bathing and swimming. In the past its hard sand made it a natural thoroughfare, and until the beginning of the nineteenth century, when the roads in the hinterland were improved, it offered travellers an attractive alternative to staircase paths. Today it still offers the opportunity to walk for miles without sight or sound of motor traffic, but the scope which the beach offers for long walks belongs more properly to the next chapter.

Returning to the town, and to the time of the early tourists, we find the Reverend William Bingley dealing with that perpetual problem for travellers: accommodation. At the beginning of the nineteenth century what was available at Harlech was still very primitive.

> The public house at Harlech, for such it can only be denominated, is kept by a civil man, called Amoyl. The provisions were indeed plain, but the beds, (only two, and those in the same room) considering the smallness of the house and the obscurity of it's situation, clean and comfortable. A guide may be had from this place, who will conduct the traveller either amongst the mountains, or over the sands to Beddgelert.

The Welsh are a naturally hospitable people, and even if facilities at some inns were not quite up to the standards which tourists were beginning to expect, then Joseph Cradock, writing in 1774, describes the noble tradition of offering a welcome to all travellers.

> An unpolished people, it is observed, have little or no curiosity, — I had seated myself by the fire-side in one of the houses in Harlech without the inhabitants expressing the least surprise at it; the guide and attendants began to be rather clamorous for some refreshment, and the people at length brought them some oatmeal bread, some porter, and stinking cheese. On my leaving the house, I believe that I gave the mistress of it more than she expected, for she immediately re-called me to share some cockles with her, that were stewing on the hearth, and while I was tasting them, she super-added a look of such native kindness and goodwill, as infinitely surpassed all the artifices of refinement.

Cradock is almost certainly wrong here; the curiosity of people who live in isolated communities is usually boundless, but so is their courtesy, and though they may long to cross question a stranger, good manners often prevents them from doing so. The inhabitants of this area were not slow to appreciate the commercial possibilities presented by these visitors from England, who were willing to travel over many miles of rough country to see their castle. In the early years of the nineteenth century steps were taken to make the accommodation at Harlech as attractive as possible. G. J. Bennett's description of the newly built Blue Lion Inn, recorded during the 1830s, shows that the hardships which the earliest tourists had suffered in order to see Wales were coming to an end.

The Blue Lion Inn, built by Sir R. W. Vaughan, for the accommodation of travellers and tourists, is most delightfully situated. A carriage road from the north leads round to the front, which faces the sea; and forming a semi-circle, permits the vehicle to drive, through a gate to the south end of the house, again into the highroad. Great taste is displayed in the erection of this building; the parapet wall, with its circular turrets, in which seats are placed for the accommodation of visitors, and the terrace with its neat shrubberies. I must also acknowledge, that the kind attention of the landlord and his servants, deserve the highest commendation.

The view from the terrace is indescribably beautiful. The sea lies stretched beneath; the majestic ruins of Harlech Castle stand upon a rocky base, frowning in rocky grandeur upon the right; and beyond, the long line of the Carnarvonshire hills project, like Cambria's lance, forbidding the waves to make further inroads upon her territories.

Pwllheli and Port Maddock are distinctly visible from this spot; and the lovers of fine prospects may remain at the Blue Lion for a week, without wishing to stray further than the terrace in search of the sublime and beautiful. The continual variety of light and shadow, with which the mountains are robed, the freshness of the air, and the solemn majesty of the ruined fortress, form altogether a volume for the mind to peruse with intense and unwearied interest.

The Blue Lion is still standing, and can be found in the main street under the name of the Plas Cafe. In fine weather it is possible to eat on the terrace which Bennett describes, and those who do so will certainly agree that he does not exaggerate its charms. The same standards of friendliness and efficiency also seem to live on today.

Catherine Sinclair also mentions this inn, and records one of those poetic images in which the Welsh language abounds; this one loses little in translation.

> We returned to the inn, which is embellished with beautiful gardens, commanding a noble view of Cardigan bay. The white and foaming waves on a shore like this are called by the Welsh 'mermaid's sheep' [defaid y fôrforwyn].

Having seen the castle, and pondered on its history, there was nothing to detain the early tourists in Harlech, but many did use it as a base from which to explore Cwm Bychan. The approach to this remote valley from this direction is as exposed and dramatic as the more usual route from Llanbedr is sheltered and tranquil. Though many of them recorded their impressions of the lake and its surrounding mountains, I can find no contemporary description of their route, so I have turned to the excellent one provided by Askew Roberts in his *Gossiping Guide to Wales*.

> Pedestrians would do well to take the walk from Harlech to Cwm Bychan. The start is up the road past the Post Office, for one mile, when the road divides, and you bear to the left until you come, in nearly another mile, to an upright stone on your right, a few yards

past which you must leave the road through a gate on your right, and your path leads direct to the mountains, which you see spread out before you. Your road now bears to the right all the way to a barn, to the right of which you pass through a gate and on to a rough footpath amongst the stones — still in the direction of the mountains. Very soon a fine panorama opens out ahead. You can see over the Cwm and Carreg-y-Saeth the higher front of Rhinog Fawr, at the lower end of which you may note (by carrying your eye over the nearer hill) the gap that forms the Drws Ardydwy, with Rhinog Fach to the right of it. Your path now descends and you shortly arrive at Gerddi Bluog, where Archdeacon Prys, who translated the Psalms into Welsh meter, was born. Leaving the house to your left you pass the gable end of a barn, let in to the masonry of which there is a tablet bearing the following inscription:—"Morgan Prys: Hydref: y: 31: 1728. W.H. Pen Saur." W(ill.) H(umphrys) was a local mason who once resided in the district. From this point, bearing left, in a few minutes you reach Dolwreiddiog farm, on the road to the lake. Take the road to the left, and you reach the lake in an hour and a half from Harlech.

Some of the paths which Askew Roberts describes have now become narrow hill roads of the type which are still a joy to walk on. An up to date description of this excursion is included in the appendix on longer walks.

One of the incidental advantages of the building of new roads is that the old ones often become quiet and neglected, providing modern walkers with the opportunity of experiencing some of the actual routes which the early tourists used in much the same way that they did. For those who would like a short and undemanding walk from the centre of Harlech, such an opportunity presents itself on the outskirts of the town. By tracing the old road to Llanfair you can follow in their footsteps and see the northern end of Cardigan Bay at its most spectacular.

Leave the main street heading south, but opposite Clogwyn Guesthouse turn up the steep hill on your left. After passing beyond the houses the view opens up to the right, and a little further along you will see a farm which looks as though it has not changed since Richard Warner passed by on the 3rd. September 1798. On that day we know that the weather was appalling, and that his party had already walked from Penmorfa, a village some way beyond Porthmadog. At Harlech they had paid a somewhat hasty visit to the castle.

Every external circumstance induced us to continue at Harlech; the wind blew an hurricane, the rain fell in torrents, and the evening was setting in; add to this too, Barmouth lay at a distance of ten miles from us. But unfortunately no beds were to be procured in the place, and we were reduced to the alternative of braving the storm, or sleeping on the floor.

Our councils are always short and decisive; we quickly resolved to disregard the weather and proceed to Barmouth. Fortifying

Snowdon from Llandanwg

ourselves, therefore, with a little more of the landlady's neat Coniac, we sallied forth to meet the rage of the elements.

The road for the most part followed the undulations of the shore, and continually exhibited to us the awful sight of an unbounded ocean, maddened by tempest, and wrapped in foam. To the left the western limb of the mountains that stretch across Merionethshire, dropping in rocky precipices and deep hollows to the strand, formed an appropriate companion to the watery element, which in the nervous language of scripture, " raged horribly " on the opposite quarter.

Amid this impressive scenery, where all was hugeness and uproar, it was not impossible to feel the religious principle powerfully within us. Each object tended to inspire us with wonder, adoration, and humility; with a full conviction of our own insignificance, and the omnipotence and immensity of that Being, " at whose word the stormy wind ariseth, which lifteth up the waves and ocean;" and who, with equal ease, " maketh the storm to cease, so that the waves thereof are still, who weigheth the mountains in a balance, and taketh up the sea in the hollow of his hand."

This wild and singular road continued quite to Barmouth,......

An account of their reception by Mrs Lowri Lewis and her staff, when they arrived wet, cold and tired at Barmouth later that evening, is given on page 100. It is certainly worth visiting the old road when there is a westerly gale blowing, just for the glory of seeing the waves breaking in a maelstrom along the whole length of Harlech beach.

CHAPTER 6

FROM HARLECH
TO TAN-Y-BWLCH

The Oakeley Arms, Tan-y-bwlch

Whesent Richard Warner left Harlech to walk to Barmouth on a stormy evening in September 1798, his experience of Wales was quite different from that of any modern visitor; even those who travel on foot. He was making his way through a country which was indifferently mapped, where he could not understand the language of the majority of people whom he met, and where the facilities which tourists take for granted today had not even been thought of. The narrow social background from which the early tourists were drawn was not the only factor which distinguished them from their modern counterparts. Though wealth and education could insulate them from many of the hardships of life two centuries ago, there were still circumstances in which they were as vulnerable as the poorest worker.

In our own time, travel is associated with luxury. We expect to be pampered and indulged when we go on holiday; to be waited on, to have elaborate meals prepared for us, perhaps a hotel room with facilities which our own home may lack. All these concepts would have been quite foreign to the early tourists, who would have servants at home who could look after them far more effectively than those they were likely to encounter at any inn, where the simple fare which they could expect to receive would not compare with their own tables. They would inevitably encounter damp, dirty, and even verminous beds in the more remote parts of the country. For them a rough road did not just mean a slow journey, but could result in a fall or an overturned carriage. Before the days of antibiotics and x-ray machines, injuries which would be considered a minor inconvenience today, could lead to fatal septicaemia or permanent disablement. Wet clothes and damp sheets were associated with pneumonia, for which there was no effective treatment, and at the end of the eighteenth century it would have been virtually impossible to travel through Ardudwy, even in a carriage, and not get wet. These tourists were quite different from the average passenger on a charter flight today. Their exploits had more in common with a modern journey to the remotest parts left on our shrinking planet than 'doing' Europe with a rucksack and a rail-pass. So however effete their prose may seem, and however conscious they may have been of their exalted positions in society, these people were tough.

Richard Warner was not the only tourist who left Harlech late in the evening to make what, by the standards of the day, would have been considered a long and risky journey. In 1798 the

Reverend John Evans had little alternative but to do the same thing.

It was now evening, and prudence invited us to make this cheerless spot our residence for the night; but the inn offered no bed, nor anything better than the dirt floor, strewed with a few rushes. This chilling idea determined us to proceed to encounter difficulties, which could we have foreseen, would have thrown an air of comfort over these unusually miserable accommodations. It was our intention to have passed the Traeth Mawr, but the sands have of late become so shifting, as to make it highly dangerous to attempt the passage when the tide is out, so we altered our course for Tan y Bwlch. With Richards [a local guide] in our van we engaged in the arduous undertaking of reaching Tan y Bwlch that night.

The route which they proposed to follow was one which made many of their fellow tourists apprehensive even in daylight.

We ascended a difficult stair-case path, up the steep side of a craggy mountain, and took a north-easterly direction over the trackless plain, known to our guide by several upright stones, called Maen hiron, and concentric circles of stones, many of them pebbles, said to have been formed for religious purposes in the ages of Druidism.

We passed the small lake named Llyn Tegwyn Isa, near which is the small village and church of Llan Tegwyn; a little farther, environed with lofty mountains is the fine lake of Llyn Tegwyn Ucha; which, from the transparency of its waters, as well as the diversity of its surrounding scenery, merits its name of Fair and Lovely. The moon was now rising, and her silver beams, reflected from the waters of the lake, heighten the beauty of this recluse but enchanting scene. The road is a narrow and dangerous path along the shelf of a perpendicular rock, on the left side of the lake, which is composed of shale or shivering slate, and many impending projections over-hang the travellers head, and threaten him with destruction. We appeared shut in by the mountain barrier, with nothing but craggy walls of rock on each side, and before us the dismal gloom of an impenetrable forest, which the pale beams of Cynthia represented in all the grotesque shapes, calculated to increase the appearance of horror, and fill the imagination with ideas of terror. Every moment we appeared to be precipitating into the lake, by the deception of nocturnal vision; while the frequent cautions of our guide, who was himself not destitute of fear, served to strengthen our apprehensions of danger. We descended into a deep glen or ravine, so thick with forest trees and underwood, as scarcely to admit a ray of light, though the night was clear, and the moon full. We passed over a black and dismal stream, called Velyn Rhyd, or the Yellow Ford, and soon got into the turnpike road, near the village of Maen Twrog; crossing a bridge of three arches over the Dwyryd, our guide with accents of joy, pronounced the inn of Tan y Bwlch!

It was two o'clock in the morning when they arrived, but they still received a warm welcome from their landlord.

A section of the road which Evans's party followed can still be found quite easily, and it provides a pleasant walk between Llandecwyn Church and Pont Felinrhyd Fawr near Maentwrog. By making this journey in darkness, Evans denied himself the pleasure of admiring the wonderful panorama which rewards anyone who climbs up to this ancient place of worship. The church stands proudly on a knoll high above the Traeth Bach, and though it is possible to drive to it, the road is a very narrow and steep one. It is surrounded by a grave-yard which forms a belvedere from which to admire the view, and in which it is a pleasure to wander. The eye sweeps from the Moelwyn summits above the Vale of Ffestiniog, past Cnicht, Glyder Fach and Glyder Fawr, Snowdon, Moel Hebog, Portmeirion and the Llŷn Peninsula. To the south Harlech Castle is seen silhouetted against the sea, with the distant coast of Pembrokeshire marking the furthest point of Cardigan Bay. Inland, stone farmhouses nestle among the woods in sheltered valleys, below the rugged slopes of the outlying peaks of the Rhinog mountains. Among the grave-stones are examples of exquisitely composed lettering, a traditional skill in this area, where the soft slate is a natural medium for artistic expression. Death would seem to have its compensations for those lucky enough to be laid to rest in such a beautiful and peaceful place.

To reach Llandecwyn Church, take either of the two roads which lead north from Harlech. Just over a mile beyond Talsarnau turn right past a modern housing development, onto the single track road which is more suitable for walking than driving.

When you reach the church, you can walk along the rough track which continues from the point where the tarmac ends. This is the old road, and it is possible to see where the metal rimmed wheels of carriages and carts have worn grooves in the living rock which occasionally intrudes on its surface. Presently you reach Llyn Tecwyn Uchaf, the scene of Evans's misgivings over the narrowness of the path and the overhanging rocks. In daylight this is free of any menace of the type which Evans describes, but a threat of another kind, which would have been unimaginable to any of the travellers on that moonlit night two centuries ago, is all too apparent. Many of the early tourists who passed this way comment on the beauty of the lake, and the clarity of its water. The water is still clear (and the fishing excellent in recent years) but the lake is disfigured by pylons carrying cables from Trawsfynydd Nuclear Power Station. It is to be hoped that by the time another two centuries have slipped by, there will be a less obtrusive means of distributing electricity than at present. Half way along the lake you pass between the stone posts of a narrow gate, on which it is still possible to detect the marks left by the hubs of carriage wheels.

For the modern walker it is not difficult to imagine a carriage jolting along this part of the track, and to wonder why there was such concern about the condition of Welsh roads in the late eighteenth century. But this would have been considered a good stretch, with the exception of the steep descent to the Vale of Ffestiniog. Those who have visited the Roman Steps above Cwm Bychan will have a good idea of what a staircase path was like, and marvel at the prospect of a wheeled vehicle attempting to negotiate such a track. Those who were unwilling or unable to walk, or ride a horse, would have found little comfort in travelling as a passenger in a carriage, as the following extract from Catherine Sinclair's journal shows. This was written after the Turnpike Trusts had improved many of the roads in the area.

Nothing would make travellers estimate more highly by the agency of contrast their obligations to Telford and Macadam, than performing a stage on the road between Dolgelly and Machlwyd, which is left almost entirely in a state of nature, without any of the modern improvements, by which tourists now always go upon velvet. The American corduroy roads are probably smooth in comparison to those we have experienced this day in going down the shelf of a mountain, on what seemed like the rough channel of a cascade, or a flight of stairs with no balustrade. I had a ready-made scream prepared for use during a progress of two miles, while it appeared that each turn of the wheels must inevitably be our last. Some philosopher observes, that life is made up of vain hopes and vain apprehensions; therefore it ought to compensate for the former being so frequently disappointed, that the latter also turn out mistaken, as was happily the case on this occasion, When we descended on the banks of the Onion [Wnion], most appropriately flowing through the land of leeks, and here fertilizing a fine productive country.

Although she is describing a stretch of road some way south of our present location, there is nothing in the early tourists' journals to suggest that this was un-typical of the condition of many mountain roads in Ardudwy at the time. Fortunately for her, by the time that she visited Harlech, the new road from Tan-y-bwlch had been built, but even so her gratitude was not entirely uncritical.

We drove on Wednesday from Tan y Bwlch to Harlech, over a new, or at least improved line of road, which possessed the rare merit, in so hilly a country, of being as level as a river. The chief objection to this modern fashion of avoiding ascents is, that travellers frequently lose the view entirely, because a wall or a hedge hems in the whole prospect; whereas formerly, taking the ups-and-downs as they came, we were amply rewarded by gaining an eye-full of scenery, such as rewarded the most tedious progress. How inseparably exertions and pleasures are tied together in this world—' ease, when courted most, farthest retires,' for as Solomon says, 'all things are full of labour,' and we generally find most enjoyment given where most trouble has been taken.

Milestone, Maentwrog

Perhaps one of the greatest contrasts between the early tourists' experience of Ardudwy, and that of our own time, is to be found in this matter of roads. When you walk or ride through the countryside, you do so as a participant in all that surrounds you, and every variation in topography has a direct and immediate effect on your progress. A steep ascent requires greater effort, passing through a wood in the bed of a valley provides cool shade, and a stretch of boggy ground is all too apparent as you sink into it. The narrow tracks which served Ardudwy two hundred years ago followed the line of least resistance, winding over passes and along the beds of valleys wherever, since earliest times, man had made his mark on the landscape. Before the days when the use of explosives made it possible to remove large quantities of rock, obstacles had to be by-passed, even at the cost of a long detour. Travellers were very much at the mercy of the countryside they travelled through.

This experience of one-ness with the landscape is still available on the single track roads in the interior of Ardudwy. You are conscious of travelling beside rivers rather than past them, and an abrupt change of direction can focus your attention on the living rock from which the landscape is made. Bare outcrops rise from the roadside, grass and heather form a corridor through which there is hardly room to pass; these roads are part of the landscape and not a feature imposed on it. If you look down on one of these by-ways you will see that it flows through the countryside as naturally as a river. Many of them are little more than surfaced footpaths, and far more is to be gained by walking on them than by edging nervously along them in a motor-car.

The main coastal route through Ardudwy has an entirely different character; it is a modern trunk road serving the needs of a community for which isolation would be fatal. The capacity for goods and people to be moved rapidly and safely from place to place is essential for a healthy rural economy, but this has only been achieved at great cost to the landscape. In spite of Catherine Sinclair's aggravating tendency to make moral comments on all that passes before her, she was an astute and observant traveller. That she should have identified one of the drawbacks of the new turnpikes so soon after they were built, and when the benefits which they brought must have been overwhelming, is as surprising as it is perceptive. If the modern tourist often feels the need to drive as far into the hills as tarmacked roads will allow, before donning heavy boots and a rucksack to stride off into the wilds, then they are denying themselves a simple if rather more arduous pleasure. For the single track roads of Ardudwy provide fine walking and are little used, making them as suitable for pedestrians as for motorists. In fact it is not unusual to wander for long periods on them without seeing a motor vehicle. It is remarkable how much of interest you can see on foot which is denied to motorists, however slowly they may drive.

For the early tourist approaching Ardudwy from the north, there was a choice of either braving the rough roads over the mountains, or risking the strong currents and shifting sands of the Traeth Mawr and Traeth Bach. The Welsh word 'traeth' means beach or shore and in this case refers to the estuaries of the Glaslyn and Dwyryd rivers, which cut deeply into the mountains of Snowdonia. The Traeth Mawr was changed out of all recognition when William Alexander Madocks completed the embankment known as the Cob, between what became Porthmadog and the Deudraeth Peninsula, in 1811. Up to that time the estuary of the Glaslyn had extended almost as far inland as the bridge at Aberglaslyn, and quite large vessels had been able to reach Llanfrothen. The vast expanse of sand which was exposed at low water, and which was later drained and turned into well cultivated farm land, provided a relatively comfortable means of travelling, provided you had a reliable guide. However dangers existed among the constantly shifting channels and soft sands, which could delay a traveller at the risk of being overtaken by the rapidly rising tide. Henry Penruddocke Wyndham sums up the dilemma which tourists faced.

As we approached Harlech, the road became scarcely practicable; it was literally a staircase path, worn on the side of a steep precipice of a craggy and disjointed mountain.......

In order to avoid the goat track of our morning ride, we returned over the sands of the Traeth Bychan, which are passable only at low water.

It is remarkable that we had never hitherto deviated from the line of our route, when alone: and that we seldom failed of doing it, when we employed a guide.

In the days before accurate road maps, visitors had to rely either on guides, or obtaining directions from locals, to whom they could not speak in their own language. This, together with the countryman's natural tendency to tell strangers what they want to hear, led to much confusion. Joseph Hucks and his companions encountered this problem while trying to find their way from Tan-y-bwlch to Harlech in 1794.

The country people here have no idea that a stranger can be ignorant of their roads; we have not infrequently asked the way, and received the answer, "that it was as straight as we could go;" when, in a very few paces, we have been perplexed by two roads, one declining to the right, and the other to the left. —— Nor have they much idea of distance; each measuring it by the rule of his own judgement and opinion. It is no unusual thing to be told, that the distance to such a place, may be about five miles [8 km], "and a pretty good step;" which pretty good step, generally proves to be about five miles more.

When Richard Warner crossed the Traethau* he did so at high tide, in conditions which must have been frightening. He also mentions that he suffered from the language problem but for another reason. The tourists' journals are remarkably deficient in

* The suffix 'au' denotes a plural in Welsh

information on the way of life of the inhabitants of the country, and although this may partly be due to the holiday-makers' habitual indifference to anything which does not directly affect their enjoyment and well-being, this is only part of the story.

Anxious to reach Barmouth this evening, we quitted Pen-morva early in the morning, crossing the mouth of the Traeth Mawr and Traeth Bychan in a small leaky skiff, with a heavy gale of wind right against us. Across this pass, however, we were safely rowed by the man and his wife who keep the ferry; the former a true Celt in stature and appearance, the latter exhibiting the remains of a beautiful person, with the eye of lustre, and the teeth of ivory, almost peculiar to the country. Unfortunately we could exchange no communication with this harmonious couple, as they scarcely spoke English. Indeed we have had occasion to remark, that much less English is spoken on the north-west coast of Wales than in any other parts.

Warner was not alone in feeling frustration at his inability to talk with many of those whom he met. Although such problems of communication were merely frustrating in the hinterland, they could lead to great danger when crossing the Traethau, as John Jackson, a London based actor with a keen eye for a pretty face, relates in a letter to the Earl of Fingall. This was written on 20th. September 1768 when he was staying with the Wynns, at Maes y Neuadd, near Harlech.

Some time ago, I was on a visit to the maritime parts of the country, where was also, among others, a lady accomplished and engaging. In her way to Caernarvon, she had to cross two dangerous sands. Though she had with her a servant and a guide, yet, even with such an escort, the passage could not be effected without some degree of hazard. My politeness impelled me to escort her to the farthest shore. We passed with great ease at low water, and I could easily have returned for dinner as I had purposed, but I went so much further, that when I got back to Penmorfa, a little village on the Caernarvonshire side, the guides refused to accompany me. Neither bribes nor threats would prevail. They understood some English, enough to say yes and no, and had learned how to count money, and the art of extortion. But they knew not enough of the language to explain the risk I should run in the attempt.

I imputed their backwardness to an un-accommodating temper and an intention to keep me at the public house all night, which, with the best entertainment which it could possibly furnish, would have been very unpleasant. I determined at any rate to have a look at the sands, and it appeared to me that the tide had made very little. I did not consider the distance I had to go, and the rapidity with which the flood rushes forward at spring tides in these western creeks. I had a stout horse, but I had pushed him hard in order to save my passage. He soon lost his feet, and, though he swam well, began to tire. I had my feet out of the stirrups, and was preparing to quit him. I could have thrown off my greatcoat, but whether or not, in my boots, I could have made the land is very doubtful. We came to a sandbank, where the horse rested and so far recovered himself as to be able to swim on. He at length felt the ground, and we reached dry land in safety. At the door of the first house, near which was a sloop upon the stocks, stood a decent-looking elderly woman. She had seen me while in the water, and was talking with the carpenter, and I afterwards understood, concerning me. I asked her if she could speak English; she said a little. I then enquired if I could pass the next traeth. Very easily, she replied, and waved her hand, as much as to say get on and loose no time. I hastened over the isthmus, perhaps three quarters of a mile across, and took the water where it was, I presume, ten feet deep. I made the marsh however, on the other side, and reached Mr Wynn's in safety.

On telling my story [to] the Welsh squire [he] was exceedingly angry and vowed revenge against the old lady for not paying greater respect, and giving better information, to his guest. The next day we went on a shooting party betwixt the traeths, and the lady was interrogated by the squire. She spoke in Welsh with great earnestness for a time. At last Mr. Wynn burst out in a loud laugh. It seemed that she owned and defended the apparent offence. For, says she, I saw him beyond all belief come through the great traeth, where nothing but the devil could have conducted him to land, and as the 'Old Gentleman' had brought him through the one I knew that he would carry him through the other. And in the conclusion I could distinguish the words 'Deawl Capten', that is, Captain Devil, very vehemently pronounced; a name with which the squire immediately dubbed me.

The appellation has been confirmed by the family and connection, which are not very confined, and, I presume, I shall retain it as long as my remembrance in the neighbourhood exists.

Jackson's imputation of dishonesty to the guides at Penmorfa was not as gratuitous as it may seem, for ferry-men in North Wales had already acquired a reputation for cheating travellers. One at Conwy had developed a reliable technique for extorting massive fares for the crossing. He would first take travellers' horses over to the farther side, and then return to re-negotiate the fare for rowing their owners across to join them.

John Wesley, forever galloping onwards intent on evangelism, had no qualms about the Traethau whatsoever.

11th. April 1749.
We reached Dolgellau in less than three hours,[from Dinas Mawddwy], Tan-y-Bwlch before noon and Caernarfon in the evening. What need there is of guides over these sands I cannot conceive. This is the third time I have crossed them without any.

The Traeth Mawr lies outside the scope of this book, and in any case the wholesale alteration of a once famous landscape, which took place here in the early years of the nineteenth century, has been fully recounted in Elizabeth Beazley's book *Madocks: The Wonder of Wales*. However the Traeth Bychan,

Ruined barn near Ynys

though tamed by embankments built by the Oakeleys of Plas Tan-y-bwlch around the same time, is substantially unchanged, in its lower reaches at least, and is still the key to one of the finest low level walks in the area. This takes you from the hamlet of Ynys along the southern shore of the estuary to Harlech Point, then south along the clean sweep of the beach to Harlech itself or, if you would like to extend your outing, onward as far as Llandanwg and Pensarn, giving about six miles (9.5 km) of easy walking. Spectacular views of Snowdon and its satellites, seen to the north east during the early stages, are complemented by Clough Williams-Ellis's eccentric masterpiece, the village of Portmeirion, which looks its best when seen clustered among tall trees on the Deudraeth peninsula just across the sands. In late spring the verges of the estuary are carpeted with sea-pinks, and at any time the variety of sea birds to be found here provides constant interest. A full description of this walk is given in the appendix at the back of this book.

There are various starting points for this excursion, and one of them will take you past the ancient church of Llanfihangel-y-traethau. Though John Evans's map of 1795 shows the old route across the sands leaving the southern shore close to the church, few of the early tourists mention it. This may be because the knoll on which it stands was still virtually an island until embankments were built in the early nineteenth century. It may even have been part of a chain of such churches, built on tidal islands, which includes St. Michael's Mount. Sheltered by vast yew trees, through which can be glimpsed the sands of the Traeth Bychan, with Snowdon beyond, the church dates back at least to the twelfth century. C. F. Cliffe makes a passing reference to it in the 1847 edition of his *Book of North Wales.*

We return to TAN Y BWLCH, and proceed to Harlech, along one of the most picturesque roads in Wales. In the beautifully situated churchyard of Llanvihangel y traethau, 1m. [1.5 km] on r. near the mouth of Traeth Bach, is a curious Norman Inscribed Stone.

The 'Wleder Stone', rising gaunt and plain above the elaborately ornamented headstones of later centuries, has an air of quiet serenity. The inscription reads; 'Here is the tomb of

A picturesque view

(By permission of Coleg Harlech Library)

180

Wleder, the mother of Odeleu, who first built this church in the time of King Owain.' This refers to Owain King of Gwynedd who reigned from 1137-1170, and according to V. E. Nash-Williams, the style of lettering used dates the stone to about 1150.

Whatever privations the early tourists suffered in order to reach this northern corner of Ardudwy, they could expect to find rest and comfort at the Tan-y-bwlch Inn. Together with the Corsygedol Inn at Barmouth it seems to have earned a reputation for providing a standard of accommodation which was far ahead of its time. But it was not the inn alone which made the area so popular. Tan-y-bwlch lay in the heart of the Vale of Ffestiniog, and this fertile and sheltered valley surrounded by steep, rugged mountains, was for many of the early tourists the epitome of 'the picturesque'. Today, although a major trunk road crosses it, one can still find much of the magic which has enchanted visitors for more than 200 years. The man responsible for making this valley a mecca for tourists was Lord Lyttleton, who in 1756 wrote enthusiastically about its beauty and tranquillity in some letters to Archibald Bower. These were published in 1774 as an appendix to Henry Penruddocke Wyndham's *Gentleman's Tour*.

Nothing remarkable occurred in our ride, until we came to Festiniog, a village in Merionethshire, the vale before us being the most perfectly beautiful of all we have seen. From the height of this village we have a view of the sea. The hills are green and well shaded with wood. There is a lovely rivulet, which winds through the bottom; on each side are meadows, and above are corn fields, along the sides of the hills; at each end are high mountains, which seem placed there to guard this charming retreat against any invaders. With the woman one loves, with the friend of one's heart, and a good study of books, one might pass an age there, and think it a day. If you have a mind to live long, and renew your youth, come with Mrs. Bower, and settle at Festiniog. Not long ago there died in that neighbourhood an honest Welsh farmer, who was 105 years of age: by his first wife he had 30 children, 10 by his second, 4 by his third, and seven by two concubines; his youngest son was 81 years younger than his eldest, and 800 persons, descended from his body, attended his funeral.

The reputation of this valley as being one of the most picturesque places in Britain quickly spread. Unfortunately the journals of the early tourists do not record whether they were attracted by the claims which Lord Lyttleton made for its beauty, or by his account of the aphrodisiac properties of its atmosphere.

One might expect that such a place would be immune from any kind of development which would alter its appearance, and that a landowner who did attempt to change it would be censured by tourists. This would certainly be the case now, but two hundred years ago things were seen quite differently. The son of a wealthy midlands landowner, Mr William Oakeley, had married into the Griffiths family of Plas Tan-y-bwlch, who owned most of the surrounding countryside, and he brought with him wealth, enterprise and a fashionable enthusiasm for agricultural improvements. In Wales in the late eighteenth century this took the form of reclaiming land from the sea by building embankments. Such activities were not seen as damaging to the landscape for two reasons: well managed farmland was considered to be more aesthetically pleasing than the sea shore, and whereas an area of countryside might be picturesque in its primeval state, there were no inhibitions about man intervening to improve on nature. By the time that Richard Warner saw the Vale of Ffestiniog in 1797, considerable changes to the landscape had taken place as a result of Mr. Oakeley's activities. Warner's reaction was surprising in the light of the attitude which tourists in our own time have to man's more recent interventions in the countryside.

Here, for the first time since we have been in Wales, we were gratified to see the spirit of agricultural improvement exerted to some extent, and with considerable good effects. The Vale of Ffestiniog consists in general of rather mossy and spongey soil, the consequence of formerly being always overflowed at spring tides. Much of the injury which these inundations occasioned to the land, Mr. Oakley determined to prevent by embankments. Having effected this, he next turned his attention to draining the ground thus secured, which he did so effectively, as to render its produce just triple to what it hitherto had been. His large drains and neat embankments rather adorn, than injure the picture; as the former are like small canals, and the latter have the appearance of raised terrace-walks, surmounted with neat white railings.

This evidence of man's ability to dominate his environment would have reassured eighteenth century tourists. But perhaps the greatest difference lay in the attitude of the agricultural improvers themselves, who were by no means ignorant of the cult of the picturesque. They were often concerned to combine enhancement of the beauty of their property with maximising their income from it. In our own time, man's manipulation of the landscape seems to have become incompatible with aesthetic improvement, so we must seek out places in remote areas like Ardudwy, where his influence is either absent or is a relic of another age, when we wish to experience pastoral beauty. Modern practices may lead to more efficient land use, but they rarely enhance the countryside. Mr. Oakeley's embankments, covered with close cropped turf, provide charming raised walkways along the river, and certainly do not intrude on the landscape.

Not only had the appearance of this valley been substantially but sympathetically altered, but there was industrial activity here as well. Richard Fenton records in 1804:

> Maentwrog Church, which we pass before we came to the bridge, is a very simple building, and has nothing without or within to attract notice. Came in to our inn at Tan y Bwlch a few minutes before dinner, much disposed to enjoy it. After dinner strolled under Tan y Bwlch house as far as the estuary, and returned along the embankment on the opposite side of the river warf, on which lay vast quantities of a delicate blue slate of all sizes ready for shipping. They are sold by the weight. They are brought from a little beyond Ffestiniog, from quarries belonging to Manchester men. Vessels of 200 tons come up the river to be loaded at spring tides, and the slates are sent down in boats to them. Return to our inn with a relish for tea, and soon after as great a relish for bed.

Until the narrow gauge railway between Blaenau Ffestiniog and Porthmadog was completed in 1836, vast quantities of slate, quarried in the Ffestiniog area, were brought down to Maentwrog by road, where it was loaded onto lighters to be transferred to larger vessels anchored in deep water; an inefficient and costly procedure resulting in considerable losses due to breakage. None of these developments seem to have affected the tourists' enjoyment of the area. The Reverend John Evans may have mis-named the valley, which is generally known as the Vale of Ffestiniog, in his 1796 description, but travel writers have always suffered from such problems.

> Nothing can exceed the beauty of this little vale of Maentwrog; it may, as Mr. Pennant observes, be justly called the 'Tempe* of Wales'. We pursued the course of the stream by which it is divided.

* *A valley near Mount Olympus, famous for its beauty.*

It is a tract about four miles in length, composed of rich meadows, whose sides are edged with thick groves, and barren rugged precipices close the enchanting scene. The little river which beautifully meanders through it, is named Dwyryd, or the Two Fords, from the Cynfal and another stream, whose name we could not learn, uniting their waters just above.

The name of the second stream is the Goedol, and instead of the fords which Evans mentions, both rivers are now spanned by fine stone bridges. This eastern part of the vale, upstream from Maentwrog, is still very much as Lyttleton and Evans described it. Although it is possible to see the valley while driving along the main road, there is a far more attractive option. A footpath leaves the A487 near the bridge over the Dwyryd at Maentwrog and follows one of the embankments until it joins the unclassified road which runs along the north bank of the river. This in turn joins the main road near the head of the valley; a walk of about 45 minutes. If you wish to make a circuit then you should turn left here, along the A496 for half a mile, when you will reach the hamlet of Rhyd y Sarn. This stretch of road is narrow, and carries heavy traffic, so some care is necessary. Beside the bridge which crosses the Afon Teigl in the centre of Rhyd y Sarn you will find a path on your left, but this has a character very different from the first part of the walk, rising high on the hillside above the valley as it winds through mixed woodland, eventually taking you back to the Oakeley Arms Hotel at Tan-y-bwlch. It is described in the appendix dealing with longer walks.

When the Reverend John Evans arrived at Tan-y-bwlch at the end of his epic night walk from Harlech, he was not disappointed by his reception.

It was now two hours past midnight, and the people had been long retired to sleep; but the landlord, when he had heard our story, with great alacrity arose, and furnished every comfort the house

185

afforded. Time had made changes here; the lady who kept this inn a short time ago, so celebrated for her attention to travellers, was dead; yet it is but justice to say, that we found the accommodation equally good, and Cartwright not behind his predecessor in point of attention and civility. This inn has been recently fitted up, in a peculiar style of neatness, by Mr. Oakeley, and forming the central house between the plain and the mountainous country, is a great accommodation to travellers.

The early tourists' references to the inn are mainly complimentary and no doubt many of them found it a welcome haven after rigorous excursions through more savage parts of the country. But even this admirable establishment had its limitations, as George Nicholson describes in his *Cambrian Traveller's Guide and Pocket Companion* of 1808.

The accommodations here are very indifferent for the pedestrian, as the compiler has experienced. The best front room was taken up by a chaise party, one facing the stables by another with horses. What then remained? why the humours of the kitchen.

It would seem that at the beginning of the nineteenth century there were already enough tourists visiting the valley to divide them into carriage trade and the rest. Indeed that indefatigable young pedestrian, the Reverend Richard Warner, had an even more unsatisfactory experience than George Nicholson. His journal reveals a courteous and appreciative traveller, always at pains to acknowledge the small kindnesses which make so much difference when visiting a strange country. Both his tours were made entirely on foot and the distances which he and his companions frequently travelled were astonishing. It is worth recording his progress during the two days prior to his arrival at Tan-y-bwlch.

OAKELEY ARMS HOTEL, TANYBWLCH,

VALE OF FESTINIOG.

THIS old-established and favourite Hotel enjoys a high reputation among Families and Tourists. Few Hotels are more favourably situated than this—on the sunny side of the far-famed Vale of Festiniog, noted for its beauty and salubrity. It is also within a short walk from the Station, on the wonderful Festiniog Railway. The Rhayadr Du and the Raven Waterfalls are only a short distance off.

The charming and extensive GROUNDS of W. E. OAKELEY, Esq., are open for Visitors staying at this Hotel.

A Telegraph Office at the Hotel. A Conveyance from the Hotel meets the Trains during the Season at Tanybwlch Station. Post Horses and Carriages for Hire.

L. J. RAE, Proprietress.

(By permission of Mrs. M. R. Lauder)

On the morning of Saturday the 19th. August 1797 the party had left Machynlleth and walked eight miles to Tal-y-llyn, where they hired a guide to escort them over Cadair Idris. The southern route which they were using is more demanding than the Pony Track which most tourists followed, but their exertions were rewarded by fine weather and a superb view from the summit. By the time they reached Dolgellau that evening they had covered twenty-four miles (39 km) over very rough country and Warner recalls:

> We reached the Golden Lion at eight o'clock, and are preparing to refresh ourselves after the severest fatigue we have yet experienced.

But by the next day he writes:

> We rose earlier than usual this morning, after a most comfortless night; during which we had been tormented with fleas, and nearly suffocated by the closeness of a room nine feet by five and a half, into which were crammed two beds and a chair. Fatigue is, indeed a powerful opiate, and we dropt asleep notwithstanding all the inconvenience of our situation. Nature however, took only as much repose as was absolutely necessary for her restoration, and we were awake and up with the first glimpse of day.

Not only had they spent a miserable night but the weather had changed. They set out in heavy rain to visit all three of the famous waterfalls at Ganllwyd, which involved a considerable detour from the main road. Still, they had the well known comforts of the Tan-y-bwlch Inn to look forward to that evening. Warner's account of what happened when they arrived, after walking a mere twenty miles, is a masterpiece of restraint.

> We were now extremely wet, and very well inclined to seat ourselves by a comfortable fire-side; you will therefore imagine our disappointment, when the host of Tan-y-bwlch inn told us we could neither be provided with a dinner, nor accommodated with beds at his house. There is a mode, you know, of imparting unpleasant intelligence, which, if it do not lessen the evil told, leaves us at least in a good humour with the person who tells it. The landlord of the Tan-y-bwlch inn, however, was either unacquainted with this art of softening the disagreeable, or at least did not choose to exercise it; for he communicated his information in a manner so ungracious, as to fix an indelible impression on our minds of his being a very surly fellow.

When Warner returned to this area the following year, it is not surprising that he chose to by-pass Tan-y-bwlch. He and his companions were now faced with a walk of a further eight miles to Beddgelert, over what was reputed to be one of the roughest and most desolate roads in North Wales. When they eventually reached the bridge at Aberglaslyn, having been hampered by mist on the higher parts of the road, daylight was fading. On such a gloomy evening, with the clouds well down over the mountains, they were unable to enjoy one of the most important examples of the picturesque on any Welsh tour.

It is remarkable that some twelve hours after leaving Dolgellau, and after the unpleasantness at the Tan-y-bwlch Inn, he still retains his enthusiasm for the scenery, although he does quote the description of Aberglaslyn gorge given by an earlier tourist (Henry Penruddocke Wyndham in *A Gentleman's Tour*) rather than providing his own. After all, considering the state of the weather, and the lateness of the hour, he could not have seen very much of it. They were still able to find the energy to examine copper workings in the Glaslyn Gorge before returning to the road which:

> .....conducted us to Beddgelert, a village at the foot of Snowdon, where civil treatment, good accommodation, and comfortable cheer, have made amends for all the inconvenience and disappointment of the last day.

His itinerary records a distance of twenty-eight miles (45 km) for Sunday 20th. August, and one might have expected his party to take things easy the next day. In fact they walked on to Caernarfon, a distance of twenty-five miles (40 km), ascending Snowdon and visiting Dolbadarn Castle on the way. In just three days they had walked 77 miles (124 km), climbed North Wales's two most important mountains, and still found time to admire all the sites of interest on their way.

In the days when Mrs Owen ran the inn at Tan-y-bwlch matters were ordered very differently, and there seems to have

189

been a warm welcome for all travellers. John Byng, the future Lord Torrington, who had been so distressed by the company he had been forced to spend the evening with in Barmouth, describes the kind of hospitality that made this inn famous. This chronic hypochondriac had just enjoyed a short walk in the Vale of Ffestiniog.

> I had, now, done enough for the morning; so I climbed up to my mountain, to enquire about dinner; an ample provision Mrs O. had provided for me - salmon, boil'd fowl, gammon of bacon, cold beef and tarts!!

This meal cost him 8d (6p), and his landlady 'Hoped there was nothing unreasonable in it'.

Close to the inn stands Plas Tan-y-bwlch, occupying a ledge surrounded by oak woods, high above the valley. This is now a study centre run by The Snowdonia National Park, but when it was re-built by the Oakeley family in the 1790s it was considered to set a standard for gracious living in this remote corner of the country. As in other places it was quite acceptable for tourists to visit grand houses uninvited, to admire their architecture, their paintings and to wander in their extensive gardens. The Reverend John Evans recalls:

> The hills are moderately high, and thrown about in pleasing variety; the sides in general are well wooded, especially to the North, being defended from the violence of the West winds. In one of these native hanging groves, strands Tan-y-bwlch Hall, the elegant seat of Mr. Oakeley; who, at a great expense, has taken advantage of the munificence of nature, by cutting walks and vistas through the woods for a considerable extent. The house peeps through the trees, and the majestic oak, and spreading beach, wave their branches in the wind over the sylvan mansion; while the meandering river widening into the estuary, called the Traeth Bach,

or Little Tide, in opposition to the Traeth Mawr, into which it opens to the South, gives a view of the ocean, and the peninsula forms a pleasing termination to the view.

In another account of a visit to Plas Tan-y-bwlch, Thomas Roscoe provides a fine evocation of the spell which the Vale of Ffestiniog cast over visitors lucky enough to stay there all those years ago.

Regaining the high road, I soon reached the pleasant and salubrious village of Maentwrog; passing through which I shortly arrived at the Caen Coed Inn — now, however, more familiarly known by the appellation of the 'Oakley Arms Hotel.'

The following morning was delightfully fine and the air invigorating. After breakfast — accompanied by a pedestrian from the Emerald Isle, who, though a previous stranger to me, I found a most agreeable and intelligent companion,— I entered the grounds of the neighbouring mansion, eager to behold the truly romantic scenery around. Few things can surpass the pleasure of a morning ramble through the woods which clothe the heights above the hall, or the splendour of the prospect from the terrace over the vale, which is delightfully enriched with every feature of landscape and of water, and forms a rich panoramic picture.

In my walk through the grounds, I observed some magnificent specimens of the rhododendron, of nearly thirty years growth, and more than forty yards in circumference; many other trees and plants seemed to grow equally luxuriantly, and both gardens and plantations were tastefully laid out, and well adapted to the soil and to the continual inequalities in the surface and the aspect. It was here that I first remarked the singular appearance of two fine young trees, an elm and an ash, which, having sprung up side by side, intertwined their stems almost from the root in so strict an embrace as to present the sylvan phenomenon of a single tree.

It is still possible to wander along the extensive network of paths created by Mr. Oakeley, to admire the huge rhododendrons in the garden and to enjoy the magnificent view of the valley from the terrace in front of the house. Maps showing the layout of the paths are available in the visitors' car park.

The Vale of Ffestiniog had everything which the pre-Victorian tourist could desire; comfortable accommodation, picturesque scenery, the opportunity to admire agricultural improvements, an ancient castle within easy reach, and that most important of attractions, a waterfall. Though this was not in the valley itself, it was only a little way south of Maentwrog on the River Prysor, with the old road to Harlech passing quite close to it. The Reverend William Bingley visited Rhaeadr Du, sometimes referred to as the Raven Falls, in 1798.

I left Maentwrog, and enquiring the road to Harlech, proceeded on my journey. At a distance of about half a mile, I crossed a small bridge, when, leaving the road, I wandered along a foot path up a wooded valley on the right, for about a mile and a half, in search of a waterfall that had been described to me, called Rhaeadr Du, The Black Cataract; but it was not without some difficulty, and after much ascending and descending, that I found it. In this cataract, which is surrounded with dark and impending scenery, the water is thrown with vast impetuosity over three black and smooth rocks, each in a different direction. Of it's height I could form no idea, as the top of the upper fall, by the winding of the rocks, was not visible from below. The rock that hangs immediately over the fall, was, from it's great height and rude form, a fine object in the landscape, and the whole of the hollow, for some distance below the cataract, extremely grand. I attempted to climb to the upper part, but the rocks were too perpendicular and slippery to attempt it without danger; therefore contenting myself with seeing as much as I could from below, I crossed the water, and crept along the shelving rocks by the side of the stream, for near half a mile. Here the banks closed in over my head, leaving but a narrow chasm, from which the light was excluded by the dark foliage on each side, and I found myself entering, to appearance, into the mouth of a deep and horrid cavern. The sides were too steep for me to think of clambering up, and except going quite back again to the cataract, I had no alternative but to penetrate this dismal place. This I soon did, for it continued but a small way; and now finding it's banks sufficiently slanting for me to ascend to the meadows above, I was not a little pleased to escape from this abode of damp and horror.

Though Mr. Bingley failed to climb the cliffs beside the falls he probably made a fairly determined attempt, as in spite of the rather staid impression his writing gives of him, he seems to have had a weakness for desperate exploits on steep and slippery rock. He once visited Snowdon in the company of the Reverend Peter Bailey Williams, rector of Llanberis, on a plant collecting expedition. While trying to reach a choice specimen on the cliffs of Clogwyn Du'r Arddwy they decided that it was less dangerous to continue upwards than to descend. The nerve racking exploit which followed earned them the accolade of being the first climbers to make an ascent on this most fearsome of Welsh rock-faces.

To find Rhaeadr Ddu, take the steep road leading into the hills beside Maentwrog Power Station, about one and a half miles west of the village. After three quarters of a mile a large notice on your right-hand-side warns of the danger of entering the river's gorge without checking with the Power Station that water is not likely to be discharged from Trawsfynydd Lake; a path leads across the field beside it to a stile. From here you descend on the left to a viewing point overlooking the falls, well out of reach of the water. If you doubt the warning about descending further, look at the tide-line of debris left high among the rocks, which indicates the level to which the river can rise.

Returning to Maentwrog there is still much to see as the Reverend John Evans points out.

Balcony, Maentwrog

The village of Maentwrog, with its white-washed cottages, is truly picturesque. It takes its name from a large upright stone, called the Stone of Twrog, standing in the centre of the vale.

Driving through the village one gets the impression of a rather grim community huddled in the shadow of a steep hill. Yet the early tourists admired this place, and if you walk along the footpath which leads downstream from the bridge, you will see why. Meadows interspersed with fine trees fill the valley floor, and the village rises behind its church against a backdrop of birch, alder and huge scots pines, the latter probably being survivors of eighteenth century plantings. Most of these houses were built in the nineteenth century, and the white-washed cottages have been replaced by taller, more prestigious Victorian dwellings. The author of *The Cambrian Directory*, published in 1801, provides a highly romanticised description of the interior of one of the original cottages.

> Passing through the village, we observed a small but neat cottage, which was rendered interesting to the way-farer by its neat simplicity. Perceiving a stand of fruit at the door, we were enticed to enter the cottage, where we found the interior of the house as comfortable as the situation was interesting. A large old-fashioned chimney corner, with benches to receive a social party, formed a most enviable retreat from the rude storms of winter, and defied alike the weather and the world:— with what pleasure did I picture,
> " A smiling circle, emulous to please,"
> gathering round a blazing pile of wood on the hearth, free from all the vicissitudes of the world, happy in their home, blessed in the sweet affections of kindred amity, regardless of the winter blast that struggled against the window, and the snow that pelted against the roof. On entering, the wife who possessed "the home of happiness, an honest breast," invited us " to take a seat" under the window, which, overlooking the village, and the dark tower of the church, offered the delights of the season. The sweets of the little garden, joined its fragrance to the honeysuckle, which enwreathed with rich drapery the windows; and here too lay the old family Bible, which had been put aside on our first entrance: we regretted not having seen the husband, whom, I make no doubt'

> " Envied not, and never thought of kings,
> " Nor from those appetites sustain'd annoy,
> " That chance may frustrate, or indulgence cloy;
> " Each season look'd delightful as it past,
> " To the fond husband, and the faithful wife."

Long before tours became the fashion, and before such romantic excesses as the passage quoted above could have been conceived, there lived in the village an honest wordsmith who left a legacy of Divine literature which will be revered as long as the Christian liturgy is observed in Welsh. We have already encountered him at his reputed birth place of Gerddi Bluog; *Lewis's Topographical Dictionary* provides a sketch of his career.

> The Rev. Edmund Prys, Archdeacon of Merioneth, one of the most eminent poets of his time, was rector of this parish for many years. He translated the metrical version of the Psalms of David used in the Welsh churches, one of which he is said to have versified every time he had service in his church, in which the whole were sung previously to their being published; and he also assisted Bishop Morgan in his translation of the Welsh Bible. He was Born in Gerddi Bluog, in the parish of Llandecwyn, in 1544, and was interred under the communion table of this church.

The old church, which many of the early tourists would have seen, was re-built in 1814 and again in 1897. Though the most recent re-modelling is unusual in design, it is admirably suited to its situation, and has retained the feeling of antiquity which the old structure must have possessed; Saint Twrog's remarkable stone can still be found in the churchyard.

At this ancient place of worship, among the picturesque woods and pastures of the Vale of Ffestiniog, with Twrog's stone reminding us of the mixture of legend and history which imbues this wonderful landscape, we come to the end of our wanderings through Ardudwy in the company of the early tourists.

Their personalities emerge from their writings in spite of their self-effacing and mannered prose. The youthful enthusiasm of Richard Warner, Thomas Roscoe's slick professionalism, the Reverends Bingley and Evans's humourless moralising, Henry Penruddocke Wyndham's sharp intelligence, John Byng's aristocratic disdain and Richard Fenton's keen forensic interest in all that he sees. But this seems to be in spite of the authors' efforts to keep self out of their writing. Most of their recollections are factual and impersonal, with only an occasional glimpse of their feelings. None of them tell us very much about their personal circumstances, and this has resulted in some tantalising mysteries.

The early tourists were strangely reticent about whom they travelled with and yet few seem to have travelled alone. We know that Wyndham was often accompanied by Sir Richard Colt Hoare, and that at different times Richard Fenton travelled with both of them. Samuel Taylor Coleridge was among Joseph Hucks's companions, but in all these cases this has only been revealed by subsequent research; the authors have not thought it necessary to tell us themselves. The Reverend Richard Warner never identifies the long suffering party who followed him for endless miles in any weather, and Catherine Sinclair only refers to the intrepid friend who scaled the ruined staircase at Harlech Castle as 'Mr. A.....'. However there is one notable exception to this reticence. The author of the *Cambrian Directory* not only names his travelling companion, but also speaks frankly about their relationship in a poem which he includes at the end of the book.

> Yes, thou hast been companion to my tour,
> And partner of my toils! hast roved with me,
> Thro' Cambria's rude and wild variety,
> And often soothed the solitary hour
> With thy caresses; yet false man can claim
> Superior reason, claim a mind enbued
> With love, with faithfulness, and gratitude;
> Love, a mere sound, and gratitude a name.
> Yes, faithful creature! and when thou art gone,
> With fond attention shall thy bones be laid,
> And a small tribute to thy mem'ry paid,

In these few words, engraven on thy stone:
" Here let in peace the faithful Sylvio lie,
" The truest picture of fidelity!"

This poem is entitled 'To My Dog', and ironically, the author published his tour anonymously.

FROM EARLIEST TIMES

Standing Stone near Merthyr

Man's development and the appearance of the landscape have been closely linked from the earliest times. When we look at an expanse of rolling moorland, we may think of it as wilderness, un-altered by human influence, but this is rarely the case. It is also tempting to think that changes which have taken place during the relatively short space of the last few centuries, which can be charted by an abundance of written material, have transformed the countryside in a more radical way than ever before; this is probably not the case either. Between the time when man first colonised the British Isles and the era when the earliest historical records were set down, successive waves of immigrants, always with new skills for exploiting their environment, brought about a transformation more radical than anything which we have seen since. The evidence of human settlement on the moors above Dyffryn Ardudwy date from the most energetic period of those changes, when nomadic hunters became settled farmers and trade routes between distant centres of population began to be established. Changes in climate were the most important single influence on the way in which primitive man could use the land..

By about **8,500 B.C.** the glaciers which had covered much of Northern Europe during the last **Ice Age** had receded, and the last remnants of the ice sheet which covered Ardudwy 18,000 years ago finally melted. The mountains had been formed very much as we know them now; but this was an age of desolate tundra grazed by deer, reindeer, musk ox and other species now associated with the arctic. Nomadic hunters followed these herds as they moved northwards in the wake of the retreating ice. Birch and willow were beginning to colonise this bleak landscape, but man left no impression on it. By **7,000 B.C.** the **Boreal** period had begun, with hotter summers and colder winters than we experience now; oak, elm, hazel and lime were forming dense forests. This was followed by the **Atlantic** period, from about **6,000-4,000 B.C.**, which combined higher temperatures with increased rainfall. Man was able to start a more settled existence along the sea shore. Not until the **sub-Boreal** period which followed, with more sunshine, did he begin to populate the higher ground which, though it is bare moorland now, was then covered by forests. After **2000 B.C.** the warmer conditions had important consequences in lands far to the south, which were to precipitate aggressive waves of migration. These people were raiders and marauders who brought with them a new technology; the smelting of iron. By **600 B.C.** another change in climate had set in, the **sub-Atlantic** period, bringing the harshest environment which Wales had known since the end of the Ice Age.

Richard Fenton's suggestion (page 111) that there was a pre-historic town on the moors above Dyffryn Ardudwy is an attractive one, but more recent research tells us that the earliest of these remains pre-date towns of any kind in this country, and that they were created during **neolithic** times, from **3,300 B.C.** onwards. To put this into the chronological context of man's history in North Wales, the earliest evidence of his presence dates from one of the warm periods which occurred during the last **Ice Age**, perhaps **60-70,000** years ago. These earliest inhabitants were not **Homo sapiens** but his ancestors **Neanderthal man** who was displaced when ice once again covered the land.

When the ice finally began to retreat around **12,000 B.C.** humans once again entered the landscape, and by **8,500 B.C.** the cave dwelling hunters already mentioned had established themselves. Little evidence of these **mesolithic** people survives as they stayed close to the sea-shore, and the subsequent rise in sea level has obliterated most traces of them. However we do know that it was during this period that these cave dwellers began to inhabit clearings in the forests as well, and that this was associated with a new way of life. Although their culture was still nomadic, **mesolithic** people made sophisticated stone tools, they felled trees, domesticated dogs, and made pottery, combining hunting and fishing with primitive animal husbandry.

Around **3,300 B.C.** a new race began to arrive in this sparsely populated landscape, and with these **Neolithic** immigrants from Iberia and Western France came radically new ideas and skills. These were the people who built the earliest of the cromlechs which can be seen around Dyffryn Ardudwy. The **Neolithic**

Revolution had reached Wales, and with it came a religion which required monuments for the dead and farming skills which led to a settled existence with permanent dwellings. But perhaps the most radical feature of this new culture was the means of the immigrants' arrival. We know that they came by sea and that their vessels were substantial enough to import cattle, sheep, corn and pigs. They were also more technologically advanced and were able to exploit the gold and copper in the hills.

From this time onwards Wales was included in a trading network which encompassed the western seaboard of Europe from the Mediterranean to the Baltic. Across the water in Ireland the same changes were taking place, with the newcomers establishing a religious centre which was to exert a wide influence in Western Europe for nearly four thousand years. During this time paganism was replaced by Christianity, which would be spread far and wide by Irish missionaries until the collapse of the **Celtic Church** at the end of the dark ages. Close ties with Ireland are an important feature of this period, and Irish influence is recognisable in the construction of the cromlechs behind the school at Dyffryn Ardudwy. These are among the earliest in Wales dating from before **3,000 B.C.** Much later, Irish monks would establish churches at places such as Llandanwg and Llanaber.

So the remains which we see around Dyffryn Ardudwy belong to two distinct periods. The first, which includes cromlechs, stone circles and cairns which date from about **3,300 B.C.** onwards, were built by settled farming and trading peoples who enjoyed a relatively peaceful and prosperous existence. The warmer **sub-Boreal** climate allowed them to move inland to the forests on the higher ground where they employed slash and burn techniques to clear land. These activities, combined with livestock grazing on the seedlings under the trees, led to the destruction of the primaeval forests which had gradually covered the land since the ice had retreated, thus producing the moorland scenery which we are familiar with today.

This change in the climate, so benign for the inhabitants of Ardudwy, was causing hardship for technologically more advanced peoples around the Mediterranean, forcing them to move northwards in search of more temperate conditions. Previous migrations seem to have been peaceful, with the newcomers finding space to settle and then integrating with the resident population, adding their new skills to the ones already established. Around **400 B.C.** all this changed. For the first time Wales was invaded, and fortifications such as Craig y Dinas and Pen y Dinas were built in response to this new threat. These hill forts, which were relatively easy to defend, provided a commanding outlook over the sea.

The time which elapsed between the end of the last ice age and the end of the dark ages is six times greater than the time which has elapsed since the Norman conquest and the present day. It is hard to know if man's development was greater during the former or the latter period.

APPENDIX II

WHO WERE THE EARLY TOURISTS?

Dates in italics indicate when the authors visited Wales. Unfortunately there are a number of tourists, including John Torbuck, about whom nothing seems to be known.

Aikin, Arthur
1773-1854
1794

Born at Warrington, the son of a well known chemist and physician. After training for the Unitarian Ministry he seems to have suffered a crisis of faith and he chose to follow a scientific career instead. His primary interest was in chemistry but he was also a botanist and a mineralogist. His *Journal of a Tour Through Wales and Part of Shropshire*, was published in 1795 when he was only 22; he was accompanied by his brother Charles who later became an eminent surgeon. In 1807 Aikin was a founder of the Geological Society. He died un-married in 1854.

Alderson, Harriet
? - ?
1818

Daughter of a Rotherham ironmaster, she married a clergyman who combined his pastoral duties with a passion for landscape gardening; to the extent that he was known to his family as 'Gardening Alderson'. Harriet seems to have been a conscientious and energetic vicar's wife who combined wealth with a keen sense of social responsibility.

Bennett, G.J.
1800-1879
1837
Born into a theatrical family at Ripon, Yorkshire. From 1813-17 he served in the navy before becoming an actor. Well known in London as a trustworthy performer of the second rank, he had a second career as a photographer after he left the stage.

Bingley, William
1774-1823
1798
Born at Doncaster and orphaned while still young, he made his tour while he was studying for the priesthood at Cambridge. This was his first book and it remained in print, in various editions, for many years. He was a prolific writer on natural history, botany and geography of whom it was said; 'His life was devoid of incident, his days were passed in compilation.'

Byng, the Honourable John
1743-(?)
1780s
His family had been associated with the navy for generations but he chose to make a career in the army, not surprisingly considering the circumstances in which his uncle, Admiral John Byng, was executed for misconduct in 1757. He may have seen active service in Germany at the end of the Thirty Years War, but by 1782 he was working at Somerset House as a tax collector. His brother, from whom he inherited the title, squandered the family fortune.

Cradock, Joseph
1742-1826

1776

His all consuming love of the stage resulted in his leaving Emmanuel College Cambridge without a degree. He became a friend of Garrick, but unlike most of this fast living circle, he is said to have subsisted on a healthy diet of turnips, roast apples and coffee, never drinking wine. Among his other publications were works on religious subjects and plays, but eventually his love of grand living reduced him to penury.

Defoe, Daniel
1661-1731

c1720

Best known as the author of *Robinson Crusoe* he published over 250 works, many of a highly political nature, and was imprisoned on more than one occasion. Though his *Tour Through England and Wales* is written as though it is the record of a single journey, it is probably based on numerous visits over many years.

Evans, John
1768-1812

1798

Probably the son of Benjamin Evans of Lydney in Gloucestershire, a clergyman. He received his degree from Jesus College Oxford at the age of 21, and although he was ordained he seems to have devoted his life to writing. The journal of his tour through Wales went through various editions and was incorporated into the thousand page *Beauties of England and Wales*, which is still valuable for research purposes today.

Fenton, Richard
1746-1821
1804-13

Born at St. Davids, Pembrokeshire to a wealthy Welsh speaking family of landowners, he attended St. David's Cathedral school and briefly worked in a London customs house before entering the Middle Temple to study law. During his time in London he became acquainted with most of the literary and dramatic celebrities of his day including Dr. Johnson, Oliver Goldsmith and David Garrick. Though he practised his profession for a while after returning to Wales, most of his life was devoted to travel and writing. He was a meticulous observer of everything he encountered, and in the early years of the nineteenth century he repeatedly left his estate in Pembrokeshire to make tours through North Wales. The wealth of records which he left at his death rival Pennant in giving an accurate picture of Wales two hundred years ago. A contemporary described him as 'a man of indefatigable industry, of a fine poetical fancy, of a very cheerful disposition, of particularly gentlemanly and fascinating manners, and a person of the best information on practically every subject'. He was a close friend of Sir Richard Colt Hoare.

Giraldus Cambrensis
?1146-1223
1188

Born at Manorbier in South Wales to a Norman father and Welsh mother, he was influenced by the progressive ideas of the former and the nationalist sympathies of the latter. Throughout a long and successful career in the church, (he became Archdeacon of Brecon at an early age) he campaigned for an independent Archbishopric of Wales based in St. Davids, but this ambition was never realised. He also travelled to Ireland and left a similar record of his experiences there.

Hoare, Sir Richard Colt
1758-1838

c1795

After being educated privately, an allowance from his grandfather provided him with the means to indulge his artistic and literary talents from an early age. He married Hester Lyttleton, (a relative of the Lord Lyttleton whose letters made the Vale of Ffestiniog famous) in 1783. After her early death in 1785 he spent most of the following five years travelling on the continent. He was a friend of both Wyndham and Fenton, who shared his interest in Giraldus Cambrensis. Though his roots were in Wiltshire, where he was active in public life, he built a summer residence overlooking Llyn Tegid near Bala.

Hucks, Joseph
1772-1800

1794

He was born into a prosperous brewing family, but his father died when he was still a child, and he was never well off. After studies at Cambridge he was called to the bar and combined his legal work with a fellowship at his old college. It is not clear how intimate his friendship with Coleridge was before their trip to Wales, but it is known that they visited Robert Southey together. The journal of his tour, which lasted for a month, was published privately and left him out of pocket.

Hutton, William
1723-1815

c1790

Born into a poor family at Derby, he described his ancestors as being remarkable for their 'honesty and supineness'. His astounding energy enabled him to make a fortune after he moved to Birmingham, but his great popularity in that city would suggest that like his ancestors, he was an honest man. When his book on Wales was published he was eighty years old and still walking long distances on his travels. As a self made man he is rare among the early tourists.

Jackson, John
1742-1792
c1770
The son of a Berkshire vicar, he was educated for the church but preferred the stage. As an actor-manager and dramatist he was associated with Drury Lane, Covent Garden, the Haymarket and various Scottish theatres. He suffered at least one bankruptcy and was described by contemporaries as being 'consumed with vanity, an indifferent performer with a harsh voice'. His letters from Wales were intended for publication.

Kilvert, Francis 1838-1879
c1870
The son of a clergyman, he was educated privately and at Wadham College Oxford. His fame rests entirely with the diaries which he kept. In 1865 he became curate at Clyro and Bredwardine in the Wye Valley, an area which has since become known as the Kilvert Country. Lack of means made it difficult to find a parish of his own, and though this sensitive and loving man formed several romantic attachments he was unable to marry until 1879. Sadly he died of peritonitis soon afterwards. The majority of his diaries were destroyed by a niece; one of the great losses to English literature.

Lewis, Samuel

d 1865

c1830

Successful London publisher who is best known for topographical works on England, Wales, Scotland and Ireland.

Lyttleton, Lord George

1709-1773

1756

His success in politics was mainly due to his connections, but he had a reputation for unimpeachable integrity, a benevolent character and strong religious beliefs which led to his being known as 'the good Lord Lyttleton'. A prolific author, who enjoyed great popularity at one time, his work was considered to be painstaking rather than original.

Mavor, William Fordyce

1758-1837

1805

A native of Aberdeen, he rose to prominence by obtaining a post at a school near Blenheim Palace and this led to his teaching the Duke of Marlborough's children how to read. An enormously successful textbook on this subject, together with the gift of a living of which the Duke was patron, established him in society. His academic qualifications seem to have been somewhat sketchy, but he enjoyed an extremely successful career as a compiler of educational books.

Parry, Edward
1798-1854

c1840

Born at Trelawnyd in Flintshire, he moved to Chester as a young man and set up business as a bookseller and publisher. He specialised in Welsh books, including his own, and took a leading role in the life of the Welsh community in the town. His *Cambrian Mirror* went through three editions and was followed by railway guides which heralded the new age of mass transport. He was also well known for his antiquarian writings in both Welsh and English.

Pennant, Thomas
1729-1798

c1775

Born into an ancient family of Flintshire landowners, he was presented with a copy of Willoughby's *Ornithology* at the age of twelve which awakened his interest in natural history. His own *History of Ornithology* became a standard work on the subject, and after its publication in 1781 his name ranked high among eighteenth century naturalists. His other publications include an account of his travels in Scotland, but a similar work on Ireland was abandoned when he failed to keep a journal during his visit because 'such was the conviviality of the country'. He was a friend of Linnaeus and of Gilbert White, who wrote his *Natural History of Selborne* in the form of letters to Pennant and Danes Barrington.

Porter, Sir Robert Ker
1777-1842

1799

Born in Dublin, the son of an army surgeon who died when he was two years old. He attended art school at Somerset House and established himself as a theatrical scene-painter. In 1800 he became famous for exhibiting a canvas 120 feet long entitled *The Storming of Seringapatam*. Thereafter he served in the army and travelled widely in Spain, Persia, Armenia, Georgia, Venezuela and Russia, where he married a princess and became one of the Czar's court painters.

Roscoe, Thomas
1791-1871
  c1835

Son of William Roscoe of Liverpool, a lawyer, banker and historian. Began to write for local magazines and journals after his father's bank crashed. He followed the career of author and translator for the rest of his long life, specialising in travel books.

Sinclair, Catherine
1800-1864
  c1830

Daughter of Sir John Sinclair, an aristocratic Scottish politician, she acted as his secretary from the age of fourteen until he died when she was 35. Thereafter she embarked on a highly successful career as a novelist, but still found time to take an interest in good works in her native city of Edinburgh. These included establishing soup kitchens for the poor, providing seats in busy thoroughfares for the weary, and building water troughs for thirsty horses. She never married.

Skrine, Henry
1755-1803
  c1795

Born into a family of Somerset landowners he graduated from Oxford in 1781. Though he was called to the bar the following year he seems to have devoted most of his life to travelling. His book on Scotland was particularly important, as even less was known to the general public about the remoter parts of that country than about Wales.

Warner, Richard
1763-1857
1797-8
The son of a respectable London tradesman he entered the church but had difficulty in obtaining preferment until Warren Hastings took an interest in his career. A prolific writer throughout his long life, he also published works on religion and antiquarian subjects as well as journals of tours in other parts of the country. An obituary described him as a man of independent thought and character.

Wesley, John
1703-1791
c1750
Evangelist, hymn writer and leader of the Methodist movement. He lived in America during the early part of his ministry and after his return to this country, following a scandal over a broken engagement, his extensive travels in pursuit of evangelism probably gave him a more thorough knowledge of the British Isles than anyone of his age. He had a reputation for having a rigid and autocratic character, but this side of his personality seems to be absent from the matter-of-fact diary entries which are quoted in this book.

Wright, George Newenham
1790?-1877
c1830
Probably born in Ireland, he received an M.A. degree from Trinity College Dublin in 1817 and was ordained in 1818. He

held various curacies in Ireland before turning his attention to writing on history and travel.

Wyndham, Henry Penruddocke
1736-1819
1774
Born into a wealthy Wiltshire family he was educated at Eton and Wadham College Oxford. Between 1765-67 he travelled on the continent visiting France, Italy, Sicily, Switzerland and Holland. In 1768 he married a Salisbury heiress, and throughout the rest of his life played an active part in the public life of his county. The Dutch artist Samuel Hieronymus Grimm accompanied him on his tour of Wales, and although his journal was published anonymously in 1775, subsequent editions bore his name on the title page. He was the author of a number of well regarded works on topographical and antiquarian subjects.

PRONOUNCING
WELSH PLACE NAMES

Welsh is often described as the language of heaven. This is not just a reference to piety but also to its great beauty as a spoken language. Sadly, when someone who is not familiar with Welsh is confronted with a name like **Dolmelynllyn** the first reaction is usually panic.

This is necessarily a very brief guide to a subject which could well occupy a whole chapter, and it does not cover all the letters of the alphabet. If you spend just a few minutes making yourself familiar with the simple rules given below, then the rest will come naturally as you hear people using the place names, and your experience of Wales will be greatly enhanced.

In some ways Welsh is easier to pronounce than English, for there are no silent letters nor are sounds often changed by the context in which letters are used. Even the apparently endless string of consonants in some words seem less intimidating when you realise that two of them, **y** and **w**, are vowels. Of these two letters **y** is the more difficult, as it is usually pronounced like *u* in *run* when it occurs in the first syllable of a word, and like *i* in *bliss* in the last. In Welsh a **w** produces the *oo* sound as in *too*. Bearing this in mind there is no problem in pronouncing **Badrwyg,** *(Bad-roo-ig)*

The letter **f** is pronounced like the *v* in *vast,* but **ff** like the *f* in *fox,* which sounds far more complicated than it really is. **Dyffryn** is therefore pronounced *Duf-rin* but **Fychan** is pronounced *Vuchan.*

Add these rules to the fact that **u** is pronounced in the same way as in *busy* (sharp as in *bliss*) and one can say **Sarn Badrwyg** near **Dyffryn Ardudwy** (*Sarn Bad-roo-ig* near *Duf-rin Ar-did-ooy*) with complete confidence.

This brings us to other double letter combinations which cause confusion, **dd** and **ll**. The former is pronounced like *th* in *thus,* (a single **d** is the same as in English) and should pose no problems. This is not so with the **ll,** which is the greatest stumbling block for non-Welsh speakers, as it has no equivalent in English. Try putting the tip of your tongue just behind your top teeth and saying *lust.* If the air passes either side of your tongue (aspiration) you are well on the way to mastering it. The most common mistake is to pronounce **ll** like *ch* in *chat.* The second most common mistake is not to ask someone to demonstrate this sound for you. We can now attempt **Llanenddwyn**; the aspirated sound followed by *an-en-thoo-in.*

Also try: **Hengwm** *Hen-goom*

    Ddu   *Thee*

    Figra   *Vigra*

    Ffestiniog *Festiniog*

    Tyddyn *Tuthin*

With these rules you will be well on your way to making yourself understood, but there are one or two other considerations which will help you to master this problem. The first of these involves two important vowel combinations:

ae and **ai** are pronounced *aye*, so **Traeth** is pronounced *Trayeth.*

au similar to the above but with emphasis on the sharp **u** sound mentioned above; **Traethau** is pronounced *Trayethaye*

Though the struggles which most of us have with unfamiliar languages can be lightened by humour it is particularly important, when in Wales, to realise that great efforts are being made to preserve the language. This was in real danger of extinction not much more than a generation ago, and it is easy to cause offence by failing to make any attempt to pronounce place names properly. If you are asking the way to **Pwllheli** then *Pelly-welly* just will not do.

Finally, Welsh is not a language which can be spoken diffidently; conviction is essential. If you try to break up long names into separate distinct syllables, delivered hesitantly, people will not understand you. So take courage and say:

Llanfairpwllgwyngyllgogerychwyrndrobwllllantysiliogogogoch.

SHELLS

These lists are taken from the 1884 edition of Askew Roberts's *Gossiping Guide to Wales.*

SHELLS FOUND AT HARLECH.

(Common ones not reckoned)

Actaeon tornatilis.   *Fusus antiquus.*   *Solen vagina.*
Cardium aculeatum.   *Fusus Berniciensis.*   *Tellina crassa.*
Cardium rusticum.   *Lutraria elliptica.*   *Venus chione.*
Ceratisolen legumen. *Pecten maximus.*   *Venus gallina.*
                              Scalaria communis

Pholas Dactylus, the European Piddock

SHELLS FOUND AT MOCHRAS.

(Common ones not reckoned.)

Actaeon tornatilis.
Apporhais pes-pelicani.
Artemis exoleta.
Cardium echinatum.
Cardium norvegicum.
Cardium pygmaeum.
Cardium rusticum.
Ceratisolen legumen.
Cerithium reticulatum.
Chiton marginatus.
Corbula nucleus.
Cylichna cylindracea.
Cyprina Islandica.
Dentalium entalis.
Fissurella reticulata.
Fusus antiquus.

Lacuna vincta.
Lucina borealis
Lucinopsis undata.
Lutraria elliptica.
Lutraria oblonga.
Mactra elliptica.
Murex erinaceus.
Nassa incrassata.
Nassa pygmaea.
Nassa reticulata.
Natica alderi.
Patella pellucida.
Pecten maximus.
Pectunculus glycimeris.
Phasianella pullus.
Pholas dactylus.

Pleurotoma nebula.
Pleurotoma rufa.
Pleurotoma turricola.
Rissoa parva.
Scalaria communis.
Solecurtus candidus.
Tapes decussata.
Tellina crassa.
Trochus lineatus.
Trochus magus.
Trochus umbilicatus.
Venus cassina.
Venus chione.
Venus gallina.
Venus verrucosa.

APPENDIX V

LONGER WALKS

Access

It is a common belief that land in the Snowdonia National Park belongs to the nation, and the public may go wherever they wish. This is not the case and one should always try to follow the public rights of way which are marked on maps. The routes suggested below do so wherever possible, and with the exception of the Traeth Bach and Harlech Beach walk, and part of the descent from Rhinog Fawr, they all follow more or less well defined paths. If you are unsure then it is best to either ask permission or seek advice.

Safety

The more demanding of these walks will take you through some of the loneliest countryside in North Wales. It is as well to bear in mind that, although this may be straight-forward enough on a fine summer day, the conditions which you will encounter in the winter or even during bad summer weather can make them very much more demanding.

<u>Always be sure that :</u>

- you tell someone where you have gone and when you will return.
- you obtain a weather forecast before you set out; 'phone Mountain Call Snowdonia Forecast on 0891 500 449.
- you carry adequate clothing and some nourishing food.
- you wear enough clothes and never become cold.
- you have a map and compass and know how to use them.
- you know what to do in the event of an accident.
- you stick to your route and report your return promptly.

<u>You should not;</u>

- embark on routes which are too demanding or will make you very tired.
- walk on your own or allow your party to split up.
- enter caves and mine workings or attempt to climb cliffs.
- be misled into thinking that descent is less demanding than ascent; this is when many accidents occur.

<u>Wherever you go follow the country code:</u>
Enjoy the countryside and respect its life and work.
Guard against all risk of fire.
Fasten all gates.
Keep your dogs under control.
Keep to public paths across farmland.
Use gates and stiles to cross fences, hedges and walls.
Leave livestock, crops and machinery alone.
Take your litter home.
Help to keep all water clean.
Protect wildlife, plants and trees.
Take special care on country roads.
Make no unnecessary noise.

This code was prepared by the Countryside Commission.

Times, Distances and Heights

The time which it takes to cover a given distance can be affected by physical fitness, the necessity of consulting the map often, roughness and steepness of the ground in descent as well as ascent, the weight of a rucksack and weather conditions. Therefore the times given in the text are only a very rough guide.

Heights are given in both feet and metres. The figures given for ascent indicate the rise from the starting point to the highest elevation without taking into account undulations.

Public Transport

An excellent combined bus and train timetable is available from tourist offices and some post offices, and this should be considered as essential equipment on these longer walks. Services on most routes are infrequent.

Maps

All directions are based on the Ordnance Survey Outdoor Leisure Series maps, which are widely available in local shops, and are easily identified by their distinctive yellow covers. It is assumed that anyone who undertakes these walks will be in possession of one of these, so the information given below is not sufficiently detailed to follow them without consulting the map.

Sheet number 18 covers the whole of Ardudwy, but those wishing to climb to the summit of Cadair Idris will also need sheet number 23. Most paths are clearly marked in green though some are shown as faint dotted lines. If you reach a point where it seems necessary to climb a dry-stone wall and there is no stile, you are lost and should back-track until you find the path again. For this reason it is good practice, where possible, to trace your progress by the position of the walls which are clearly indicated by thin black lines.

For those who require a more comprehensive directions for walks, Richard Sale's detailed and very informative *Best Walks in North Wales*, published by Constable, describes several excursions through Ardudwy similar to those included here.

1 Ascent of Cadair Idris 2927 ft (893 m)

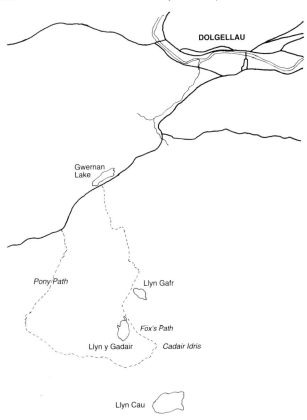

Time: Allow at least four hours for the round trip to the summit.

Ascent. 2419 ft (737 m)

The early tourists would have left Dolgellau on the old Tywyn road, complete with guide, pony and an elaborate picnic, and the distance they would have to cover to reach the summit would be about 6 miles (9½ km). Their route was known as the Pony Path and parts of it are still marked as such on the Ordnance Survey map today. For the modern tourist the distance walked is likely to be shorter, as it is now possible to motor as far as Tŷ Nant at 508 ft (160m). After you pass Llyn Gwernan look out for a bridge with a car park on your right. The beginning of the path is clearly marked.

The first stage is a delightful amble through hazel woods beside tumbling mountain streams, until the ground steepens for a while before reaching a gate onto the open hillside. Here the angle of ascent eases again, but further on another short steep section leads to the saddle between Pen y Gadair and Carnedd Lŵyd. By this time a spectacular view has opened up behind you, encompassing the Arennig mountains, the valley of the Eden and the Rhinog peaks, with a glimpse of Cardigan Bay to the north west. A few yards further on the path crosses to the other side of the ridge, opening up an equally impressive view to the south, while it continues to rise steadily until it veers left to the very edge of the sheer northern precipices overlooking Llyn y Gadair. From this point onwards particular care should be taken if the weather is bad, for the path stays close to the cliffs up the final steep boulder slopes to the summit cairn. (see Arthur Aikin's description of the view on page 111).

The Fox's Path is an alternative route of ascent but is probably more appropriate for descent because of the steep and loose nature of the ground. The exact point at which it leaves the ridge, about 250 yards east of the summit, is hard to identify in mist despite its being marked by twin cairns. As it is the only safe route of descent on this side of the mountain it is wiser to return by the Pony Path if you are uncertain. In any case it is only suitable for those who are sure footed and properly shod. Below Llyn y Gadair fork left to return to the Pony Path or continue down past Llyn Gafr to rejoin the road by the Gwernan Lake Hotel.

WARNING! The paths described are well used and easy to follow in fine weather, but Cadair Idris has a reputation for attracting cloud, and it is essential to have your wits about you at all times. Please heed the following cautionary tale which Frances Kilvert includes in his account of the ascent.

As we went towards the mountain my old guide told me how Mr. Smith (Tom Colborne's clerk at Newport), was lost on Cader Idris some six years ago. He was on a tour in N. Wales, walking with his knapsack and had come to Machynlleth. He wanted the guide on the Machynlleth side to go over the mountain with him and offered him 2/6 [12½p]. The guide refused, saying his fee to go to the top of the mountain was 5/- [25p] and if he went down the other side it was 10/- [50p]. Moreover the guide strongly advised Mr. Smith not to attempt the ascent alone that evening, for night would soon fall and the weather was bad. However Mr. Smith persisted in going on and the guide went a little way with him to put him in the road. Two days after this the guide was in Dolgelly and meeting my guide, old Pugh, he asked if he had seen anything of the gentleman who had crossed the Cader from Machynlleth to Dolgelly two days before. Pugh said he had neither seen nor heard anything of him although he had been up Cader Idris twice that day, one time being late in the evening. So they supposed Mr. Smith had changed his mind and had gone down from the top of the mountain to Towyn. But six weeks passed. Nothing was heard of him and his wife grew very uneasy. His brother came to Machynlleth, Towyn and Dolgelly to make inquiries but could hear nothing, and the mountain was searched without result. Mr. Smith disappeared in September, and in the following May a man was up on Cader Idris looking for a quarry. He heard his dog bark suddenly and looking over a precipice he saw a dead body. He hurried back to Dolgelly and fetched a doctor and policeman and the coroner, and Pugh came along with them. When the body was turned over Pugh was horrified. He said he never saw such a sight and he hoped he should never live to see such another. It was what had been Mr. Smith. It was a skeleton in clothes. The foxes and ravens had eaten him. His eyes were gone. His teeth were dashed out by the fall and lay scattered about the mountain. His head was bent double under him and crushed into his chest so that his neck was broken. The only piece of flesh

Mr. Smith's Hat?

remaining on the bone was where the coat buttoned over the chest. One leg was gone and one boot. Pugh looked up and saw something white lying on a ledge above where the body lay. It was his Knapsack. When it was brought down there were his things, his papers, his money. Then his stick was found. And some months afterwards Pugh found his hat. Pugh said he had probably tried to come down a short way to Dolgelly and must have fallen down a precipice in the mist and growing darkness. He showed me the place where the body was found. He found the marks the body had made in falling and knew exactly the place it had fallen from. He had carefully measured the distance and declared the body must have fallen 440 yards [402 m].

Sadly lives are still lost on Cadair Idris in much the same way.

2 Tal-y-bont to Bontddu.

Time: From Tal-y-bont to Bontddu allow at least 3½ hours.
There are bus services at both ends of this walk and a train service at Tal-y-bont.
Ascent: From Tal-y-bont to the cairn on Llawllech: 1739 ft (530 m)

Start at the bridge over the river Sgethin at Tal-y-bont and follow a well used path on the left bank until you emerge on a small road by a cottage; here you can obtain refreshments in the summer. Cross Pont Fadog and then go up the hill on the other side until the road ends at a gate. Beyond this are two tracks. The one on the right leads towards Bwlch y Rhiwgyr and is mentioned in chapter 4 as one of the alternatives for returning from Carneddau Hengwm. Take the other one past Llyn Erddyn, with a fine view of Craig y Dinas (see page 73), to the junction with the path from Pont Sgethin to Bontddu, where there is a standing stone. This path is not marked in green on the map but as a faint dotted line.

Before turning right, and starting the steep ascent of Llawllech, you may wish to go down and see the lovely old pack horse bridge over the Sgethin; a perfect place for a picnic. The next stage up to the cairn on the ridge above Llyn Erddyn is hard work, but provides an ever more dramatic outlook over the moors which were once the home of some of the earliest inhabitants of Ardudwy. At the first bend you will find a touching tribute to an indomitable lady who seems to have had little trouble with this ascent. When you reach the cairn there is a *coup de theatre* which will banish all memory of this long slog. Suddenly Cadair Idris appears looking its most splendid, with the Mawddach estuary spread out below and the houses of Dolgellau, almost hidden by trees, in the distance.

Go through the gate by the cairn and begin the descent. From here the walking is a delight, as the path contours round the hillside over rolling downland and then follows a smooth ridge until it joins a road at the edge of the woods above Bontddu. Continue as far as a telephone box by a bridge, where you can take a path on your right which follows the bank of the river. Presently this joins a track which passes the Clogau and Figra mine, and just before Figra Bridge you turn left onto a narrow path through a kissing gate. This later becomes sensational when it follows the side of a gorge, until you pass through a narrow alley by a house to join the main road at Bontddu.

3 The Roman Steps, Rhinog Fawr and Drws Ardudwy

Times: From Cwm Bychan car park to the top of the Roman Steps (Bwlch Tyddiad) and back allow at least 1½ hours. To reach Cwm Nantcol from Cwm Bychan allow at least 3 hours. From the car park to the summit of Rhinog Fawr, returning by Gloyw Lyn, allow at least 3 hours.

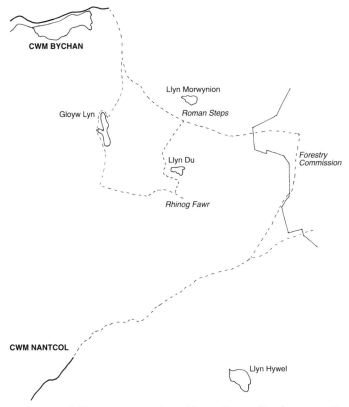

There is no public transport in either Cwm Bychan or Cwm Nantcol.

<u>Ascents From Cwm Bychan</u>: to Bwlch Tyddiad 918 ft (280m): to the summit of Rhinog Fawr 1837 ft (560 m)

Many people will be content to walk to the top of the Roman Steps and enjoy the view from there. For those who would like a longer and more demanding excursion here are two attractive alternatives.

You can reach the summit of Rhinog Fawr by taking a very rough path to the right by a wall just before you reach the top of the Roman Steps. This route is steep in places, but unless you are riding a horse like Mr. Bennett (see page 128) it is not particularly hazardous. Llyn Du, the small lake close to the summit, is a pleasant spot to rest before starting the final ascent; or even for a swim when coming down. But in bad weather this can certainly be a wild and desolate place, and I have often been glad to find the lake so that I could fix my position accurately on the mountain. If you wish to avoid scrambling up the loose scree just below the summit, turn right on a level path for a short distance, and then left up easier ground.

When I first walked in the Rhinog mountains, in the nineteen fifties, there were very few paths, and even those owed more to the activities of sheep and goats than to human feet. Now there are too many, causing problems when navigating in mist, as they constantly divide and fade away. In such conditions it is essential to carry a compass.

There are various possibilities for the descent, the most attractive, perhaps, being to visit Gloyw Lyn. Leave the summit on a path which follows a well defined ridge to the south west. This is not marked in green on the map but as a faint dotted line. Near a large cairn, cross a ladder stile over a wall. Ignore a path which you will see in the distance crossing the moor below you in the direction of Gloyw Lyn. Carry on down towards Cwm Nantcol for a few hundred yards until you can make your way over level ground to a sheepfold at map reference 645290. There is no path between the point at which you leave the Cwm Nantcol path and the sheepfold, but from here a well used one will take you over another ladder stile and down a rocky rib to the west shore of Gloyw Lyn.

Follow the western shore to the northern end of the lake, where a steep and stony path, which is not a right of way, descends towards Cwm Bychan. To find the correct route continue round the end of the lake, and a little above it, until you see a path which will lead you back to the bottom of the Roman

Steps. This is marked in green on the map. Much of this walk lies over very rough ground and is difficult to follow.

It is also possible to make a direct descent from the summit of Rhinog Fawr to Drws Ardudwy by a very steep path. This would require careful route finding in poor visibility and should in any case be treated with some respect.

If you wish to walk from Cwm Bychan to Cwm Nantcol via Drws Ardudwy, without ascending Rhinog Fawr, then continue over Bwlch Tyddiad (the top of the Roman Steps) to a ladder stile which takes you into a conifer plantation. Presently you will reach a forest road where you should turn right, and not long afterwards right again, at a cairn with a pole on top. This path is faint and overgrown in places, but it will lead you back onto the open hillside. Follow a path which contours leftwards, and is somewhat indistinct in places, until it merges with another one just before you reach a large cairn. From here the going is either rough or boggy but never dull, with glimpses of the green pastures in Cwm Nantcol framed by the massive portals which give this pass its name.

4 Llanbedr to Maentwrog

Times: from Llanbedr to Talsarnau allow at least 4½ hours and 6½ hours to Maentwrog power station (Pont Felinrhyd-fawr).

Ascent: see below.

This walk is too long to describe in detail, and in any case it is probably better to depend on the map as the route finding in some places requires great care. Likewise no figure for ascent is given as the degree of fitness required to complete a walk of this length would make this consideration irrelevant.

The effort is well worthwhile for the spectacular views of the Rhinog range in the early stages, and of Snowdonia in the later stages. The sea is a constant presence to the west. There may be

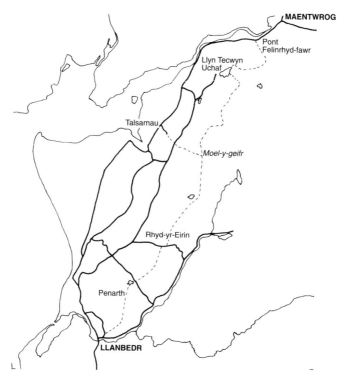

some satisfaction in feeling that you are using these paths for their original purpose; to get from place to place rather than for a gentle stroll.

If you have a car to park it is better to do so near the centre of Llanbedr village. Take the road sign posted Cwm Bychan, and at the war memorial turn left. When you reach a white cottage you will see your path rising steeply through a wood on your right. Your first objective is a farm called Penarth nearly 1¼ miles (1.9 km) NNE of this point. Shortly after passing it you will reach a road where you turn right and then left past Tyddyn Rhyddid, heading for Ffridd Farm which is 1½ miles(2.4 km) NE of Penarth. This section makes heavy demands on map-reading skills and involves some rough walking. With care, all the stiles and gates will be found.

Cross another road, turning right and then immediately left, past Rhyd yr Eirin, and the route finding becomes less demanding for a while. You are now making for Moel y Geifr farm 2½ miles (4.2 km) NNE of the point where you crossed the road. From here you can either descend to Talsarnau in about an hour by the path which leads down past Tynybwlch to Soar, or you can continue to C'aen-y-bwlch Uchaf where more decisions must be made. The Llandecwyn area is criss-crossed by a maze of paths many of which are hard to follow. Perhaps the simplest course is to head for Llyn Tecwyn Isaf, though this will involve you in a steep re-ascent to reach Llyn Tecwyn Uchaf. An alternative is to attempt to follow a higher but somewhat indirect route. From whichever direction you reach the lake be sure that when you have passed it and come to a forestry road, you turn right to Cae'n y Coed, where a steep but attractive path will take you down to Pont Felinrhyd beside the power station.

Refreshments, both liquid and otherwise, can be obtained in Maentwrog and there is a bus service along this road.

5 Harlech to Cwm Bychan.

<u>Time:</u> For the round trip from Harlech allow at least 4½ hours.
<u>Ascent:</u> From Harlech to the highest point above Cwm Bychan, 951 feet (290 m)

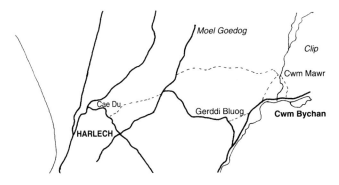

233

With Mr Roberts's directions (see page 162) and the map it is easy enough to find your way from Harlech to Cwm Bychan, but today it is a matter of following a combination of tiny lanes and footpaths.

From the hills above Harlech you obtain a completely different impression of the Rhinog peaks. When approaching them from Llanbedr they are not seen at their best until you are among them; from the coast they form a distant silhouette on the horizon. Once one has ascended to the open moorland above Harlech, with its standing stones and scattered farms, you are looking into both Cwm Bychan and Cwm Nantcol simultaneously. The depth of these valleys gives scale to the summits which seem to spread from horizon to horizon. A detailed description of Cwm Bychan is given in Chapter 4, and for those who wish to return on foot to Harlech without covering too much of the same ground twice, a suggested route is given below.

The Post Office has moved and Barclays Bank now occupies the site mentioned by Askew Roberts; it is the steep road beside this which you should take. The first section above Harlech is hard work, but as Catherine Sinclair primly observes, 'we generally find most enjoyment given where most trouble has been taken'. The reward will be clear if, as you toil up the hill, you glance over your shoulder from time to time.

Continue up the road until, a little way beyond a house called Cae Du, you can turn left onto a path between stone walls; the first part of this is not marked green on the map. Pass between two houses and a little way beyond them you will come to a kissing gate at the top of a field. Take the track which leads to Garth Mawr and by the farm buildings turn left across a field. Cross a stile marked by a white post and ignore another stile which is now facing you. Turn right and then left to find a none too conspicuous stile at the top right hand side of the enclosure which you are now in. From here the way to a stile which crosses the fence beside the road (where it joins a wall on your left) is quite straightforward.

Turn left and if you wish to follow exactly in Askew Roberts's footsteps then take the road which forks right to reach Gerddi Bluog. This house has been greatly altered since he passed this way over a hundred years ago. It was rebuilt by the architect Clough Williams-Ellis, the creator of Portmeirion, and from the front has the appearance of an Elizabethan mansion. On your right is a completely new farm-house which is a supreme example of the care which some local people are prepared to take to preserve the character of their countryside. You will still find Edmund Prys's inscription above the hayloft door of the last byre on your left.

Continue a little further down hill until you reach a footpath on your left, which leads to Dolwreiddiog, where you will join the Cwm Bychan road. Turn left to reach the lake.

For a less pastoral but far more dramatic approach to Cwm Bychan, take the left fork at the road junction by the standing stone. Keep to the road until you see a track on your right, about ¾ of a mile (1.3 km) further on, where a no parking notice is painted on a rock. A mile (1.6 km) from the road you will reach the path mentioned in the description of the walk from Llanbedr to Maentwrog. Ignore the ladder stile on your right and make for the one straight ahead. Before long Cwm Bychan will appear as a breath-taking panorama of precipices, with the lake nestling below Carreg y Saeth and the Roman Steps clearly visible winding up Bwlch Tyddiad. The way from here to Cwm Mawr, about ¾ mile (1.3 km) eastwards, is marked by a succession of ladder stiles and is easy to follow, except where you cross a wall on your right and then almost immediately cross the same wall again on your left. There is a bridge across the river a little way above the house at Cwm Mawr.

There are obvious advantages in making a round trip and this can be done by leaving the lake by the road and taking the path at Dolwreiddiog which leads up towards Gerddi Bluog.

6 Traeth Bach and Harlech Beach.

Time: Allow at least 3½ hours to reach Harlech station from Talsarnau (3 hours from Llechollwyn). Add another hour if you are continuing to Pensarn. There are bus and train services at both ends of this walk.

Ascent: insignificant.

This walk may not be possible at high tide and is best undertaken when you know that the tide is falling. A sign which

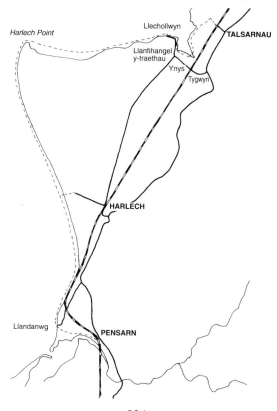

you will pass at Ynys gives the time of high water, and providing that you cross the sands between Llechollwyn and Harlech Point more than three hours before this, you should experience no problem. However you will have to ford the small streams which cross the sands and this will involve removing your footwear if you are not wearing wellington boots. Signs beside the road at Ynys give warning of the dangers of high tides and strong currents; car drivers who intend to park at Llechollwyn should bear these in mind as the road can be flooded at the highest tides. Where you begin this walk depends on the means of transport which you are using; the following description assumes that you will be leaving your car at either Pensarn (where parking can be a problem) or Harlech, and travelling by public transport to Ynys, Tygwyn or Talsarnau. At the time of writing there is a rumour that Tygwyn halt will soon be closed, but until this unhappy event comes to pass leave the train there. A short section on a busy main road will bring you to the hamlet of Ynys, where you turn right and immediately find peace and quiet. Those with cars will identify an obvious alternative when they consult the map.

If you decide to start from Talsarnau, which makes the walk a little longer, you will be rewarded by spectacular views over the salt-marshes. From the station follow the track across a field to the embankment beside the estuary, then turn left. When you reach Ynys you will see a small sign which gives the time of high water on your right, at the end of a tall building. If you wish to visit Llanfihangel-y-traethau follow a footpath across the fields on your left.

Continue to the end of the road and then walk down onto the estuary. Head for the northern end of the most distant sand-hills which mark Harlech Point. Part of this area is a nature reserve, so due consideration should be shown for the varied and abundant wildlife which you will encounter.

The point, when you reach it, is a wilderness of sandhills, saltmarsh and sea, where it is rare to see another living soul. It is also a major collecting point for flotsam and jetsam, the tide-line piled high with every imaginable item which has fallen or been dumped into the sea. In these eco-conscious times this fascinating clutter is considered to be untidy and well meaning groups seek to neaten things up.

The tide-line has always been the place where evidence of man's relationship with the sea has accumulated; only the materials have changed. An empty hand-cleaner jar (polythene) with instructions in Russian, may lie beside a wrecked rowing boat (fibre-glass) with the name of an Irish port on its splintered transom, within a few feet of a fishing float (polystyrene) with specifications embossed on it in Spanish, or a complimentary shampoo canister from a French cruise liner. When I last walked this way I carried home the most beautifully figured pieces of teak I have ever seen; once the thwart of a dinghy. Other finds have included a glass fishing float and a dolphin's scull, immaculately cleansed and whitened by the action of sand and surf.

With the wind behind you it is an easy stride down the beach to the path which leads through the sand-hills to Harlech, but for those who wish to extend their experience of this glorious coast, and do not mind scrambling over boulders for a while, it is possible to continue to Llandanwg, with the added attraction of pausing at the excellent Maes Cafe behind the beach. From here, suitably rested and refreshed, it takes only a quarter of an hour to reach Pensarn by the footpath which runs across the close cropped grass beside the Artro estuary.

7 The Vale of Ffestiniog.

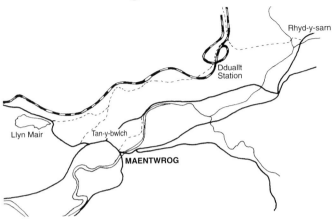

Time: Allow at least 3 hours for the round trip from Tan-y-bwlch.

Ascent: From Rhyd-y-sarn to Dduallt station 427 ft (130 m)

If you are starting from Maentwrog or Tan-y-bwlch, follow the directions given on page 185 until you reach the bridge at Rhyd y Sarn, where a green sign guides you onto a driveway. This soon becomes a delightful footpath through oak woods leading to a bridge over the Goedol, which cascades through a deep gorge; without irony this scene can be described as truly picturesque. A steep climb through conifer plantations brings you out onto the open hill-side, but here there is a note of discord. For just where you would expect to get your first view of the valley spread out below you, the eye is captured by a menacing shape half hidden by the woods to your left. This is Trawsfynydd Nuclear Power Station, designed by Sir Basil Spence, whose masterpiece was the Cathedral at Coventry. He hoped to solve the problem of blending a major industrial building into this unspoiled landscape by employing the same proportions and profile as one of Edward I's castles. Looking across the valley this intention is clear, but whereas the ancient castles do not dominate their surroundings but blend with them, Spence only seems to have been able to capture an impression of brutal strength. This was the work of a great and sensitive architect, who believed that the creation of beauty was a prerequisite of his calling; but great works are so often the product of great risks taken by their creators. His later life was haunted by the knowledge that he had failed in his intention, and that he had introduced something horrible into the Welsh countryside when he had sincerely hoped to preserve it from ugliness.

Up to this point the path has been easy to follow; now some attention to the map is required to find Dduallt Station on the Ffestiniog Railway. Here it is worth making a brief detour to the viewpoint which is signposted from the platform. When you return to the station, cross the track, turn left under a bridge and then almost immediately left again opposite a stone with 'Not Up Hill' written on it. The close cropped grass in the small sheltered meadows here make them look like lawns divided by natural rock gardens. Presently, for the first time, a spectacular view of the valley appears, before you drop down to Plas Dduallt.

In front of this ancient house a sign attached to a huge Scots pine directs you towards Tan-y-bwlch, and beyond this point there are various ways to return to the valley. After passing a cottage on your right and a foot bridge, a steep path running beneath some telephone lines offers a not particularly attractive opportunity to descend to the road. Just a little further on the way forks, and by keeping to the right you can reach the main road at Llyn Mair in about 20 minutes. The left fork leads more directly to the Oakeley Arms; but beware! The original footpath marked on the map has disappeared under a sea of conifers. An obvious alternative presents itself, and apart from a steep descent beside a cottage deep in the woods, there is no difficulty in finding the way providing one occasionally glances at the map.

If you prefer to walk in the opposite direction it is better to start from Llyn Mair as the path behind the Oakeley Arms is difficult to follow from this direction.

8 Complete Tour Through Ardudwy.

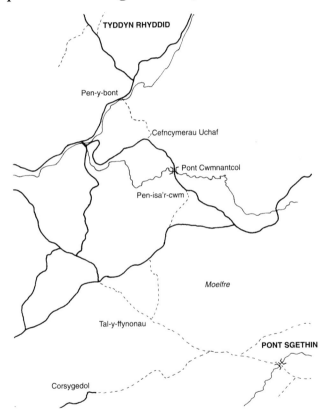

By joining routes 2 and 4 it is possible to travel from the Mawddach estuary to the Vale of Ffestiniog almost entirely on paths. This provides an extremely energetic day's walk of some ten to twelve hours and involves the use of the following linking route.

From Bontddu cross the Llawllech ridge as described (in the other direction) under Route 2, and descend to Pont Sgethin. Cross the bridge and when you join a hill road turn left. Presently a track by a wall on your right will allow you to skirt the lower slopes of Moelfre and reach a small road which leads towards Cwm Nantcol. Just before the second gate on this road turn left onto a path which will take you to another road in the bed of the valley at Pen-isa'r Cwm. Turn left along this road although there is a path which goes straight on. By doing this you will pass over Pont Cwm Nantcol, one of the highlights of this wonderful valley. At Cefncymerau Ucha take a path to the right to reach Pen y Bont on the Cwm Bychan road. Turn right and then, at a signpost to Harlech, turn left to find the track to Tyddyn Rhyddid. Follow the directions given in Route 4 from here onwards.

For those who prefer the mountaintops to the moors and valleys, a similar route which involves ascents of most of the peaks in the Rhinog Range is described in Richard Sale's book *A Cambrian Way*, published by Constable.

INDEX

244